Followers
of the Way

15 The Chambers, Vineyard
Abingdon OX14 3FE
brf.org.uk

Bible Reading Fellowship is a charity (233280)
and company limited by guarantee (301324),
registered in England and Wales

ISBN 978 1 80039 162 8
First published 2017
Second edition published 2022
10 9 8 7 6 5 4 3 2 1 0
All rights reserved

Text © Simon Reed 2017, 2022
This edition © Bible Reading Fellowship 2022
Cover illustrated by Ben Bloxham

The author asserts the moral right to be identified as the author of this work

Acknowledgements
Scripture quotations are taken from The Holy Bible, New International Version
(Anglicised edition) copyright © 1979, 1984, 2011 by Biblica. Used by permission
of Hodder & Stoughton Publishers, an Hachette UK company. All rights reserved.
'NIV' is a registered trademark of Biblica. UK trademark number 1448790.

Every effort has been made to trace and contact copyright owners for material
used in this resource. We apologise for any inadvertent omissions or errors, and
would ask those concerned to contact us so that full acknowledgement can be
made in the future.

A catalogue record for this book is available from the British Library

Printed and bound by CPI Group (UK) Ltd, Croydon CR0 4YY

Followers
of the Way

Ancient discipleship for modern Christians

Simon Reed

Contents

Acknowledgements

This book had to be lived before it was written. No one should ever walk through life alone, so I need to say thank you to various people who are, or have been, part of the journey: Ray Simpson, Graham Booth, Penny Warren and all the members of the worldwide Community of Aidan and Hilda for lighting up the path; Peter and Dorothy Neilson and Emma Loveridge, for insight and help in some difficult times; St Luke's Church, Orchards, in Johannesburg, for your wonderful and enthusiastic embracing of *Creating Community*; the Church of the Ascension, Ealing and St Mary's, West Twyford, for your constant support and encouragement as I've worked this stuff out both at home and away; and the most important people of all, Alison and Riley, and of course Emma, who we always remember. This book is dedicated to you all, with thanks. I couldn't have got this far without you.

Introduction

It was the year of the floods. Large areas of south-west England were underwater after weeks of rain, but in Scotland the rain had fallen as snow and the mountains were plastered in white. We were climbing Ben Lawers, which, at just under 4,000 feet, is one of Scotland's top ten highest mountains. The clouds had closed in and we only knew we were on the top when we couldn't climb any higher. The summit marker was buried under feet of snow and we carved out a hollow to drink tea and eat Snickers. The cold wind had already blown snow over our tracks, so we took a compass bearing to follow the easiest way down again. And that's where it got interesting.

In a white-out, white cloud meets white snow and sometimes you can barely even see your feet. As we ploughed on down, I felt the angle getting steeper than I was expecting. Suddenly someone shouted, 'There's a drop in front!' A moment later came a second shout: 'It drops off on both sides!'

We stopped immediately. One of our number switched on his GPS navigation device to fix our position. Two of us – traditional navigators – scrutinised the map to see where we had gone wrong. Quickly we spotted it, a tiny feature on the map, but clearly showing two small cliffs shaped like an arrowhead just off the left side of the ridge. We had walked to the edge and stopped just before we reached the drop. A moment later, and to our great relief and satisfaction, the GPS confirmed our old-fashioned map reading. Even with a compass, in the poor visibility we had veered slightly off course. The solution was simple – backtrack up and left and get back on the ridge top. Within minutes we were back on course and another great day in the hills was heading for a safe conclusion.

I love living in a world city, but at least once a year I go away to spend time in the mountains. Some people think we're crazy, but it's actually safer than crossing the road, and much depends on knowing what you're doing. One of the essential skills is navigation – knowing where you're going, how to get there, how much progress you're making and how to get back on track if you get lost. I wonder how many of us can apply the same set of skills and knowledge to being a Christian. Do we know exactly where we're trying to get to and how to get there? Do we know what we mean by following Jesus, and do we have any way of knowing whether or not we're making progress?

In 2013 I wrote a book called *Creating Community: Ancient ways for modern churches*.[1] I wrote about my experiences as a church leader in trying to help people to connect more deeply with God and to connect God with every part of life. I explained how my immersion in Celtic Christian spirituality, through my membership of the international Community of Aidan and Hilda, led me to insights that were known and practised in the early church but which seem to have been forgotten for over a thousand years. In particular I described how living by a Way of Life, being accompanied by a Soul Friend and sharing in a rhythm of prayer revolutionised my understanding of how we live as disciples of Christ and create deep and lasting Christian community.

The impact of the book amazed me. People wrote and told me that some of what they learned from the book was life-changing. People started calling me to speak about it in various places in the UK and abroad. As I have travelled and read and reflected, while still grappling with the challenge of leading a small church that is desperately trying to grow, I have been struck by just how many Christians are wrestling with the fundamental questions of what it actually means to be a disciple of Jesus Christ, and how you go about it in a sustainable, lifelong way. More than ever, I believe our spiritual ancestors had vital insights that we urgently need to rediscover. That's what this book is about. It will be a lifelong journey, but it will also be a life-giving journey. It's time we got started.

1

What is discipleship and why does it matter?

'Houston, we have a problem…' Those few words to NASA's Mission Control marked the terrifying realisation that Apollo 13, the 1970 mission to the moon, was in serious trouble. A faulty oxygen tank had exploded, affecting not just the air but also the power supply of the spacecraft. Not only were the three astronauts not going to the moon, but there was no guarantee that they would make it back to earth alive. Just like Apollo 13, there are warning lights going off all around the Christian church, especially in the western world. So, what's the problem?

It's an understatement to say that we're not living in happy times. Since 11 September 2001, everyone has become horrifically familiar with the idea of holy war. We have seen large areas of the Middle East brutalised by a new wave of religious fundamentalism. Inspired by this, others have brought acts of mass murder to cities, concert halls and beaches around the world. In 2016, the United Kingdom went through a messy divorce from the European Union. A few months later, the United States elected a new president expressing some of the most extreme and provocative views ever held by someone in that position. The aftermath of both decisions has been deep and sometimes violent divisions, an upsurge of racism and deep fear among minorities. No one imagined that in 2020 the world would grind to a halt as a global pandemic swept the planet, killing (to date) well over six million people. No one imagined that in 2022 a fullscale war would erupt in Europe causing shockwaves across the world. These are not happy times.

For many years, western Christians have been trying to come to terms with the ending of what we call Christendom, the way in which for some 1,500 years the values of our civilisation have been shaped, at least in theory if not in practice, by Christian beliefs. Much as some people would like to hold on to the past, this era is now over. Back in the 1990s, the crime writer P.D. James commented that the only shared morality we now have is that we're against racism. In the current political and popular landscape, it is doubtful whether even that is true any more. It has always been hard to measure exactly how many people have an active connection with some kind of church. What we know today is that in the UK it is significantly less than ten per cent, and that this has declined steeply in the last 30 years. The USA is going in the same direction. What is less often realised is that, in the last 200 years in Britain, there never was a golden age in which 'everybody went to church': at the start of the 20th century, a census in London revealed that only one in five working-class people, the largest social group, went to church at all.

Today, therefore, we find ourselves as Christians not only trying to break out of decades of decline, but also having to establish our credibility in relation to all the other major world faiths, and most of the minor ones too. In recent years, we have also had to respond to an aggressive atheism which argues that there is no place for religion of any kind, except possibly in private, misguided, personal beliefs. Violent funda-mentalism, mostly from religions other than Christianity, has fuelled this, but we have not helped our own case when some Christians have supported political and social causes that have encouraged racism and other forms of prejudice. In the past few years, then, like Apollo 13, our crisis-stricken craft seems to have drifted through the dark, with every kind of expert trying to get us back on course.

Recently, there seems to have been a breakthrough in identifying what the main problem is. According to Bishop Graham Cray of the Fresh Expressions movement, '*discipleship is the most strategic issue facing the western church today.*'[2] In a recent study of how a wide range of British churches go about sharing the good news of Jesus, the authors noticed that 'time and again the subject of discipleship has emerged in conversation', and with it a sense that many of our churches are not very good at helping people to become 'genuine and lifelong disciples'.[3] Veteran US church researcher George Barna puts it more bluntly: 'Almost every church in our country has some type of discipleship programme, or set of activities, but stunningly few churches have a church of disciples.'[4] Laurence Singlehurst, former director of Youth With A Mission (YWAM), England, highlights why this matters: 'Discipleship is on everyone's agenda. Denominations and churches realise that in today's culture, who we are speaks a great deal louder than what we say.'[5]

If you're not a church leader, this might all sound like the kind of thing you're glad you don't have to worry about! In fact, it concerns every one of us in our day-to-day lives. Week by week, you might be sitting listening to a talk in your church, or in a group discussion in someone's home, or on some kind of Christian course like Alpha. Hopefully you're enjoying it. But, at the same time, you're wondering how it relates to the difficult situation in your workplace, the struggle to spend enough time with your family, the talk you heard about the environment which left you concerned but confused about what to do, how to share something about your Christian faith with your Muslim neighbours without offending them, and the fact that for months now you've just felt tired all the time because of all the stuff going around in your head. Then there's all this political stuff that you're not sure you understand, but you wonder how on earth your Christian faith might help you make sense of that. Now and again, you hear good ideas that inspire you to grow as a Christian, but there never seems to be a way of following through on them properly. You feel that somehow God ought to be relevant to all these things and able to make a difference, but too often it just doesn't seem to happen.

The problem is this: so many of us have been told that we are, or ought to be, disciples of Jesus, but no one seems able to tell us exactly what this means or how to do it in a sustainable way that connects with all the stuff going on in our lives, not just the church bits. The consequences are huge. If we believe that God should somehow make a positive difference to every part of our lives and that does not seem to be happening, we live with disappointment and can easily end up blaming ourselves. If we are not shown that the goal of Christian living is to bring everything in our lives into relationship with God, we can end up being the worst kind of Sunday Christian who makes all the right spiritual noises but effectively lives the rest of the week as if God did not exist. Not only are we then missing something vital, but non-Christians quickly spot the gap between what we say we believe and what we actually do and are unimpressed. All around the world, for a whole host of reasons, ordinary Christians and church leaders are concerned about these issues, and again and again they bring it down to one word: discipleship.

It's often rightly said that if you aim at nothing, you're sure to hit it. So let's start right at the beginning by asking what being a Christian is all about. I am writing this as a church leader. I became a Christian as a teenager thanks to school friends who were open about their faith and not afraid to challenge my scepticism. Since then, I've been involved in helping people find faith in Christ and then grow in that relationship for pretty much all my adult life. Paul sums up the goal of his life when he says, so simply and powerfully, 'I want to know Christ' (Philippians 3:10), but along with this goal for himself he has a goal for other people, to which he devotes his life: 'It is he [Christ] whom we proclaim, warning everyone and teaching everyone in all wisdom, so that we may present everyone mature in Christ. For this I toil and struggle with all the energy that he powerfully inspires within me' (Colossians 1:28–29). That is the best summary I know of what Christian ministry and mission, and for that matter Christian life, is all about. It also raises the question of what we mean by 'mature in Christ'. What does this goal look like? What is the target at which we're aiming? I would suggest that *maturity in Christ means connecting more deeply with God and connecting God with the whole of life.* And that is exactly what being a disciple of Jesus is all about.

How often have you walked past something so often that you no longer even notice that it's there? Let's remind ourselves, before we go any further, that *Christianity is centred on Christ Jesus, Jesus the Messiah, Jesus the world's true king.* In John's gospel, Jesus makes a truly astonishing claim, to be heard against the background of different movements within Judaism, claims of the Roman emperor to be a god and the competing claims of the many other religions of the ancient world: 'I am the way, and the truth, and the life. No one comes to the Father except through me. If you know me, you will know my Father also. From now on you do know him and have seen him' (John 14:6–7). I imagine a moment of stunned silence as Thomas tries to process this answer to the question he had just asked, and Philip struggles to find the words to ask Jesus what he means. Yet in the early years after Jesus' resurrection, what we now know as Christianity was first called 'the Way' (Acts 9:2), but this Way was more than just following a teacher and his teachings, essential as this is to our understanding of what discipleship is all about. Reflecting upon who Jesus is, Paul wrote to the Colossians that 'he is the image of the invisible God, the firstborn of all creation' (Colossians 1:15). Put simply, if you want to know what God is like, look at Jesus. But that's only half of what Paul is saying.

The other half is this: if you want to know what human beings ought to be like, also look at Jesus. Saying Jesus is the firstborn is not implying that God created Jesus or that there was ever a time when Jesus did not exist. In the ancient world, the firstborn son of a king would share and exercise his father's authority, and that is what it means here. But to speak of being the image of God ought to take us right back to the beginning of the Bible where we read that 'God created humankind in his image, in the image of God he created them; male and female he created them' (Genesis 1:27). Biblical scholars have endlessly debated what exactly being made in God's 'image' means, but one of the most helpful explanations is to know how images were used in the ancient world. Kingdoms or empires could cover thousands of miles with communications only as fast as a horse and rider. Rulers exercised power by appointing governors to whom they delegated their authority. As a sign of this they would build a statue, an image of themselves, in every local centre. As human beings, made in the image of God, we are created to be entrusted with the task of helping all creation to live and grow in harmony with its creator. The biblical word 'dominion' (Genesis 1:26) is not about domination but cultivation. Sadly, it shouldn't take more than a moment to realise how far short of that we have fallen.

The story of the Bible is the story of God's rescue plan for us and for all creation, and that story comes to its climax in the death and resurrection of Jesus. Commenting on Colossians, N.T. Wright puts it like this: 'Humanity was made as the climax of the first creation... the true humanity of Jesus is the climax of the history of creation, and at the same time the starting-point of the new creation.'[6] It has often been said that New Testament ethics, in simple terms how we should behave as Christians, can be summed up in four words: be what you are. We are God's image-bearers, created to live, and to help everything in all creation to live, in harmony with our creator. To learn how to do that, we have to look to the one person who bore the image perfectly: Jesus. That is what being a disciple, a follower of Jesus, is really all about.

There is just one snag in all this. Outside of the gospels and Acts, the word 'disciple' does not appear in the New Testament a single time. Maybe that is one reason why for too many years too many Christians have produced a version of Christianity that focuses on our *personal* relationship with God and our *personal* guarantee that through Jesus we will go to heaven when we die. How we live in this life in this world, and how we relate to the rest of society and all of creation, has come a poor second, and we have too often ended up claiming to follow Christ but actually following the crowd. American scholar Michael Wilkins, in his comprehensive study of discipleship in the New Testament, helps us see what we have often misunderstood.[7]

In the first place, Acts, which was written after most of the New Testament letters, happily uses 'disciples' as an alternative word for 'Christians' (Acts 11:26), showing that this idea didn't simply drop out of use. In fact, it was also used extensively in early Christian writings after the New Testament. More importantly, even if the word itself is absent, the idea of discipleship can be found deeply embedded in the New Testament letters. The first letter of Peter sets out the idea of Christ as our 'example, so that you should follow in his steps' (1 Peter 2:21). The first letter of John picks up the same idea: 'Whoever says, "I abide in him," ought to walk as he walked' (1 John 2:6). Paul captures both of these ideas in his letters. 1 Thessalonians is basic Christian teaching written to a group of Greeks who were new believers, just weeks after they had come to faith. At the very outset, Paul reminds them how 'you became imitators of us and of the Lord' (1 Thessalonians 1:6). He urges the Corinthians, 'Be imitators of me, as I am of Christ' (1 Corinthians 11:1). In Ephesians, a letter almost certainly meant to be read around a whole group of churches, he speaks in the same breath of God and Christ, urging his readers to 'be imitators of God… and live in love, as Christ loved us' (Ephesians 5:1–2). What does it mean to live as a Christian? Paul's answer is simple: be like Jesus; imitate him.

We have a target. To be a Christian is to be a disciple of Jesus, a follower of his Way, one who walks as he walked and follows his example, one who seeks to be an imitator of him. In doing that we are fulfilling the very purpose for which God 'rescued us from the power of darkness and transferred us into the kingdom of his beloved Son, in whom we have redemption, the forgiveness of sins' (Colossians 1:13–14). That purpose is nothing less than restoring us to our rightful place as God's image-bearers. 'Discipleship is about a divinely inspired and divinely infused wholesome humanity that seeks to live generously and graciously in harmony with God and the whole of creation.'[8] If we rediscover this vision of what being a Christian, or for that matter being a human being, is all about, and set out on a lifelong journey to connect more deeply with God and to connect God with the whole of life, we cannot not become better people, living better lives in a better world. Who on earth would not want that? The next question is how we go about it.

To think about:

- For you, what is the most positive thing about being a Christian?

- What do you personally find most difficult about living as a Christian?

For a group:

- What areas of life do you think Christians sometimes find hard to connect with God, and why do you think this is?

2

The way to be a disciple

'Discipleship? Oh, yes, we did that about three years ago. It was a good course. This year we're doing creation care.' I read that just yesterday in the newsletter of a well-known mission organisation. The author was the latest in a long line observing our confusion over what discipleship is all about and our difficulty in enabling people to become genuine disciples of Jesus. He highlighted not just 'the rampant materialism of "Christian" Europe', but also, horrifically, 'the genocide of "Christian" Rwanda,'[9] as examples of what happens when we get it wrong. This is not just a western problem. It matters everywhere that people who call themselves Christians also act like it and do not allow themselves simply to drift passively along with the current of the society around them.

If Christian mission and ministry is really all about helping people to connect more deeply with God and to connect God with the whole of life, then closer observation suggests that most of the ways we go about achieving this are at best limited in their effectiveness. This came into fresh focus for me on a rare Sunday off about three years ago in the relaxed setting of a family service in a nearby church. Their minister was away too, leaving a group of enthusiastic parents to organise some very informal all-age worship for the small congregation still there in the summer holidays. It was not the kind of day to expect anything especially profound, but rather to enjoy what was there. Yet a phrase in the closing prayer after the talk stuck in my mind. The speaker asked God to help us all 'grow in faith'. I found myself wondering what precisely she meant by that. Did it mean coming to a deeper trust in God? If so, that wasn't really what the talk had been about. Did it mean growing into a deeper relationship with God? That seemed more in keeping with the rest of the service. If so, I wondered, how would we know that was happening, and what would we expect to be the impact of that on our lives and on our world?

I have sometimes been accused of overthinking things, and you might suspect this is an example of that, but for me it highlighted the question I left hanging at the end of the last chapter. Many of us have an instinct that our lives would be better if we were increasingly able to connect more deeply with God and to connect God with the whole of our lives, but even if we're able to express it as clearly as that, we do not have a clear and sustainable way of achieving our goal, and so with varying degrees of disillusionment or disappointment we so often settle for something less.

All these reflections gathered impetus a month or two later when I was talking with the minister of another local church as he was going to lead their evening service. 'How's it all going?' I asked. 'Oh, it's really exciting,' he said. 'Tonight we're about to begin a discipleship course.' 'What's that going to consist of?' I asked. 'It's ten weeks long,' he said, and, as if that explained it all, off he dashed, Bible in hand. I would genuinely have liked to know what was going to be taught in that course, but beyond that I had a much more pressing question. If discipleship is about nothing less than our whole life, and if living as a disciple of Jesus is a lifelong process, how on earth are we even going to begin to address that in ten weeks, and what are we going to do to sustain people on their journey when the course has ended?

Go to almost any church and the default method for helping people to grow as Christians is the sermon, or, if we want to be less formal, the talk. It's amazingly enduring given what a negative image this form of communication has. 'Don't give me a sermon!' people say; 'Don't stand there preaching at me!' Yet for all that we're told that it's out of date and irrelevant, we still use it. In work settings, we often listen to pitches and presentations, albeit with pictures, bullet points and video clips, but still basically someone talking to us. Last summer, I went to a political rally where an audience of several thousand listened enthusiastically to, in effect, five or six consecutive sermons lasting in total over two hours. I have heard some truly dreadful Christian preaching, but I have also heard talks that have been genuinely life-changing, where people have become Christians right there and then, or heard something from God which caused them to think and act in a completely new way. Good preaching, birthed in prayer, using every communication skill we have, explaining the Bible and helping listeners to see how it connects with their lives, still has a vital place in Christian life and growth. Please pray for the preachers you listen to and give them positive feedback to help them to do better.

Yet sermons and talks alone are not sufficient to give us anything like all we need to grow as Christians year on year. It does not take much thought to see why. Fifty years ago, committed Christians went to church two or three times on a Sunday. Today they will probably go two or three times a month. This is nothing to do with a decline in commitment. The demands of work, family and children's sport mean that many of us find our weekends eaten up by demands on our time over which we feel we have little control. The days when a preacher could say, 'Starting from where I ended last week' and expect more than half of their congregation to have been there are long gone. That is why, wisely, many churches have for decades tried to build up a range of activities outside of Sundays to help people to grow as Christians.

Courses are very popular. Probably the most well known is Alpha, which, from its initial expansion in the mid-1990s, has now run in over 100 countries and 112 languages, with over 27 million people having taken part. Alpha, as many of you will know, is a Christian basics course, designed to help people explore Christianity in a friendly, relaxed and open way, and there's no question that it has helped tens of thousands of people to begin their journey with God. For many people, Alpha is a wonderful experience. I remember someone who came to one of our courses saying that Alpha should be compulsory for everyone. The problem that has followed it all the way along, though, is what to do when Alpha ends. The common answer seems to be: either stay involved as a helper, which can be very beneficial, or else go on and do a different course to learn about some different parts of Christian life. There are lots of alternatives to Alpha, each with their own distinctive approach to presenting Christianity. Some try to address the 'what next?' problem by a series of follow-up courses. The more conservative evangelical Christianity Explored course[10] follows its seven sessions (plus away day) with an eight-session Discipleship Explored course. Pilgrim, the Church of England's successor to Emmaus, sets out not just to help people come to faith but also 'aims to equip people to follow Jesus Christ as disciples in the whole of their lives'.[11]

There's a lot of good Christian teaching in each of these courses and in many others you can find online or in Christian bookshops. The drawback to all of them is what they are: courses. Each of them offers you vital skills for Christian life, but none of them can do more than set you off on the journey, or offer you a refuelling stop along the way. Assuming you like courses and that you have time to go to them, they offer you great input and encouragement, but after that you are on your own again. They are good for a time, but discipleship is a lifelong journey, not a series of short courses.

That's why many churches have a small group structure. They recognise that Sundays aren't always an easy time to get together, and that courses are good while they last but inevitably come to an end. Instead, there is an invitation to get to know a smaller group of people over a longer time, to develop lasting relationships and to walk our journey with God together. Alison Morgan is certain that belonging to a small group is absolutely essential to growing as a disciple. 'It seems odd,' she says, 'to suggest that this can be done in any other way than that in which Jesus and the apostles did it: by gathering people together into small fellowship groups.'[12] In *Creating Community*, I briefly discussed the cell church approach whereby church is remodelled around weekly small groups which come together from time to time in larger celebrations.[13] I suggested this can be very hard to implement unless you are starting a church from scratch along these lines, and today it seems to be less talked about as a way forward. Along similar lines, and quietly growing under the radar, are a multitude of 'new monastic' communities, or missional communities, which have a strong emphasis on hospitality and meeting in homes. There is something very exciting going on here, but many of these groups are still very small, and it remains to be seen how they would function with larger numbers.

There are lots of good things to be said for small groups, and when they are functioning well they can be immensely life-giving and life-changing. They do however have one very significant drawback. Even in churches with a very well developed small-group structure, rarely do more than 50 or 60% of the church membership belong to a group. Some people belong only for a time, while others never will. Long working hours, or shift work, the demands of school-age children – including helping teenagers with homework – and the difficulties of travel in the evening for older people all take their toll. For some people, it is also a question of temperament. They are comfortable talking one to one or with a couple of friends, but find discussion in a group terrifying. Groups are great, but groups are limited. I know churches whose leadership passionately believe in the value of groups but simply cannot make them work. In my own setting, we generally meet once a month because that is the level of commitment our busy members feel they can make. If belonging to a small group is essential to our growth in discipleship, then large numbers of our church members, large numbers of committed Christians – and maybe you are one of them – are going to get left behind.

As I've said already, I am a church leader and I have been involved in Christian ministry for most of my adult life. Giving talks and leading courses is something I do all the time, along with encouraging people to meet in small groups. All of them are good things but I have come to discover that there is something even better for helping people to connect more deeply with God and to connect God with the whole of life in a sustainable, adaptable, lifelong way.

Some years ago, I became interested in Celtic spirituality, the distinctive expression of Christianity which spread throughout the British Isles from the fourth to the eighth century. Some of us, if we learned anything about Christianity at school, will have been told that Christianity came to Britain with the Romans and was reintroduced by Augustine's mission sent by Pope Gregory in 597. The reality, as many historians now recognise, is that Augustine was a missionary to London and the southeast, but there were already Christians in the British Isles, especially in the west and the north. These Celtic Christians had never been part of the Roman Empire. Ireland was converted to Christianity without a single martyr, and Irish influence spread into Scotland through the work of gifted and highly motivated leaders like St Columba, who founded the Christian community on the island of Iona which sent missionaries into the Scottish mainland. In the early seventh century, a group of missionaries was invited into northern England by the Christian King Oswald of Northumbria, the realm which at one stage extended from the Scottish Borders down to the English Midlands. They were led by a missionary bishop called Aidan who based himself on the island of Lindisfarne, now known as Holy Island. From there, Celtic missionaries worked down into the Midlands and East Anglia, while others were effective in Cornwall, Wales and Cumbria.

This is not an academic history lesson. We live at the end of Christendom, in a time when we're a minority within the British Isles. For that reason alone, it's important and inspiring to revisit the stories about how these islands were transformed from paganism to faith in Christ, and to see what we can learn from them. There are other reasons too. The Celtic expression of Christianity somehow managed to combine many different streams of the Spirit that have become separated in the second- and third-millennium church. They had a Catholic emphasis upon the sacraments and the incarnation, an Evangelical emphasis upon the scriptures and mission, a Pentecostal familiarity with healing, prophecy and other workings of the Holy Spirit and an Orthodox rootedness in God as Trinity. If we want to connect with God in his fullness and to bring him into life in all its diversity, the Celtic Christians have a lot to teach us.

My exploration of Celtic spirituality led me to join the Community of Aidan and Hilda (**aidanandhilda.org.uk**), a dispersed, inter-denominational and international network of Christians committed to applying the insights of Celtic spirituality today. I am now one of the three Guardians who have oversight of the Community, and as a result I have friends all over the world. Our community is not perfect, yet, significantly, in an age in which the church in the western world is declining, it is growing. Some people join us because they see an opportunity to grow as Christians, which their local church doesn't seem to offer. Others come because they are disillusioned or repelled by conventional church but still want God and still want community.

Nevertheless, we are a dispersed community and despite local groups in the UK, many of our members do not see each other for months if not years at a time, and I do not see them.[14] For all that, what I see when many of us do meet together, once or twice a year, is a group of people who are deeply serious about their pursuit of God and deeply committed to exploring and applying the implications of that in every area of life. There is also, despite the distances, helped of course by electronic communication, a deep sense of connection with one another. We may be dispersed but we feel ourselves, profoundly and immediately, to be one body.

I believe in the importance of preaching, I love putting on courses and I promote home groups, but my experience among the busy, committed people of my two west London churches was that these three things were not adequate to help people grow as disciples in the sense of that word which I described in the previous chapter. As I explained in *Creating Community*, I began to ask myself what it was about the Community of Aidan and Hilda that seemed to allow it to achieve this. I realised that the Community had at its core three practices which we, like most third-millennium churches, were missing. These were *sharing a Way of Life, journeying with a Soul Friend* and *joining in a rhythm of prayer*. In the previous book, I introduced all three, but in what follows I want to concentrate on the first, living by a Way of Life (which also includes in it journeying with a Soul Friend), because I've come to believe that it's absolutely vital and essential to the process of truly realising what it is to be disciples of Jesus.

If you want to go on a journey, you need a map. If you want to make a cake, you need a recipe. If you want to build a house, you need a plan. It's exactly the same with being a disciple of Jesus. We need to know what we are trying to do, how to get there and how to measure our progress along the way. This is precisely what a Way of Life is all about. You would think that no one in their right mind would go out into wild or mountainous areas without a map and compass, but again and again I meet people who do. On one occasion in England's Peak District, I met two walkers striding purposefully in the opposite direction. 'Is this the Pennine Way?' they asked. 'I'm afraid not,' I replied. 'Are you sure?' they said. I pointed to our location on my map and then to a path. 'You're meant to be going north, up here, and the map shows the ground dropping away steeply to your left. As you can see, where we are now, the ground is dropping away to your right. You're actually going east, not north!' Most people, whether or not they are walkers or climbers, have no problem seeing that venturing into the unknown without a map is not very smart. Yet that is precisely how many of us go about living our lives as Christians.

Depending on your church background, the standard answer to the question, 'How do we know what to believe and do as disciples of Jesus?' is going to be either to follow the teachings of the Bible, or to follow the teachings of our church (which hopefully in turn are rooted in the Bible). That's a good answer as far as it goes. Yet the Bible is a very big book. I sometimes ask for a show of hands in churches, and it is pretty unusual to find more than one in four people who have read the entire Bible. So how can we be following its teachings if three-quarters of us have not even read all of it? Even if we do reach the point where we have read every book, there is still the question of learning how it all fits together and how God's big story, in all its twists and turns, is meant to influence and guide us. The answer, worked out by the early Christians, but embedded in both Old and New Testaments themselves, is to work out and live by a Way of Life.

Put simply, *a Way of Life is a simple and memorable set of guidelines to help us to get an idea of what being a disciple of Jesus looks like in our time and setting, so that we can progress towards our goal and keep on track if we start to wander.*

This practice, also known as living by a Rule of Life, is first described in the oldest reform movement in Christianity, the radical monastic communities which formed in the Egyptian, Syrian and Judean deserts from the third century onwards. As Christian faith grew and became more popular and socially acceptable, it seemed to be becoming diluted. The desert Christians wanted to go back to the challenging teachings of Jesus, and although some of their practices on occasions went to extremes, which we would regard today as bizarrely strict, people who visited their communities described them as being like heaven on earth. The reason for that was that these people were dedicated to working tirelessly against their ingrained sinful selfishness in order to be more completely full of love for God and other people. Joining these communities was hard, and throughout history the monastic calling has always been one for only a minority of Christians. Nevertheless, they were highlighting something vital. The very word 'monk' comes originally from the Greek word *monos*, meaning one. The monk is a person who lives for God alone. Fourth-century Christian leaders like Athanasius, Basil the Great and John Chrysostom saw monasticism 'not just as a special form of the Christian life but as the actualisation of what was in principle demanded of all Christians'.[15] Basil guided communities of monks, but wrote books about their way of life aimed at all Christians. The extent to which this became standard practice is revealed in the historical account of one of the original Lindisfarne missionaries, Bishop Cedd, who worked in what is now Essex. Cedd 'gathered together a multitude of Christ's servants and taught them to observe the discipline of a Rule, so far as these rough people were capable of receiving it'.[16] Teaching a Way of Life was the Alpha of Celtic evangelism. It was for everyone.

You might wonder therefore why the term Way or Rule of Life does not appear in scripture. Rather like the Trinity, the word itself is not there, but the idea very much is. The first famous example can be found in the Old Testament in the book of Exodus. As you read that book, you notice that God didn't simply rescue his people from Egypt in order to immediately relocate them in the promised land. A relatively short journey takes a whole lot longer because God's intention along the way was always to spend time re-educating them so that they would understand what it was to be his chosen nation, and eventually a light to all the world. Israel ended up with a full and complicated set of laws, some found in this book and others in Leviticus and Deuteronomy. They cover not just worship but personal morality and a legal code for the whole nation. As we know from the New Testament, the law required trained and qualified teachers to interpret and apply it. There was no way that ordinary Israelites could get to grips with all of it. That is why, in Exodus 20, God gives them the ten commandments. If you pause to consider what they cover, they basically fall into three sections: relationship with God; relationship with family; relationship with other members of society. They are a Way of Life to enable ordinary Israelites to know the guidelines that would enable them to live in faithfulness and integrity with God and one another.

In my chapter in Ray Simpson's *High Street Monasteries*, I showed other less well-known examples of this in the Old Testament, but the New Testament example with which most people will be familiar is Jesus' famous sermon on the mount (Matthew 5—7). Biblical scholars agree that Matthew presents this as the set piece of teaching by Jesus on how to be a disciple. What we find in it is a large section reinforcing and reinterpreting the ten commandments. Once we learn that first-century people had far better memories than we do, we can see that again this is a section of teaching to be memorised in order to be followed as simple guidelines for being followers of Jesus in first-century Palestine. If we break down the areas that Jesus addresses, we find that it is roughly the same three: relationship with God; relationship with family; relationship with other members of society. Again, in *High Street Monasteries*, I showed how Paul does exactly the same thing in many of his letters to the newly founded churches in other parts of the Roman Empire. He addresses similar issues, but with different applications to suit their settings.

Here is the Way of Life we follow in our church. It is based closely on the one followed by the Community of Aidan and Hilda, which I learned to follow. A growing number of Christian communities today follow a Way of Life, some quite similar, others with their own distinctive emphases. No Way of Life can ever claim to be perfect or to cover everything, but I would strongly suggest that if you are trying to put into practice something like the following, it is highly unlikely that you will *not* be connecting more deeply with God and connecting God more completely with the whole of your life.

Our Way of Life consists of ten waymarks:

1 Be a lifelong learner
2 Journey with a Soul Friend
3 Keep a rhythm of prayer, work and recreation
4 Live as simply as possible
5 Celebrate and care for creation
6 Heal whatever is broken
7 Be open to the Holy Spirit and listen
8 Pray for good to overcome evil
9 Pursue unity
10 Share Jesus and justice

We also have what we describe as three life-giving principles which underlie and run through each of the waymarks. They are simplicity, purity and obedience.

In the following chapters, I am going to describe and explain each of these waymarks with some ideas about how to put them into practice. After that, I am going to explain the three life-giving principles. Really, they ought to come first, but it is easier to understand them once you see how the waymarks work. Finally, I will show you how to put all this into practice and to start following a Way of Life for yourself.

To think about:

- What does growing as a Christian mean in your life?

- What are you doing to help you to achieve that growth (and what else could you do)?

For a group:

- How can we help each other to grow on our personal journey with God?

3

Waymark one:
be a lifelong learner

Jesus said, 'Take my yoke upon you, and learn from me... you will find rest for your souls' (Matthew 11:29). The traditional definition of a disciple is one who learns.

We learn from the Bible and from creation. At the heart of our Way of Life is learning from God through daily Bible reading, and also through study, meditation and any other means of creative engagement with the scriptures. The Bible also urges us to consider God's creation and to draw lessons from what we see there.

We learn from other people and from our life experiences. In particular, we seek to learn from the lives and examples of the Celtic saints – the founders of the church in our islands, and from people of all ages whose examples illuminate our Way of Life. We celebrate the lives of these saints and regard them as our companions and encouragers (Hebrews 11:1—12:2). Since all truth is God's truth, we seek to increase our knowledge and understanding of all things that are life-enhancing and which enrich our God-given personalities and gifts. We seek to grow in knowledge, not for its own sake but that we may live more wisely and fully.

There are five ways in which we can learn.

1 Studying the Bible

We've said that to be a Christian is to be a disciple of Jesus, a follower of his Way, one who walks as he walked and follows his example, one who seeks to be an imitator of him. At its most basic, then, discipleship involves learning about Jesus in order to be like Jesus, and the starting point for that learning is always the Bible. Christians hold a variety of views about what we mean when we say the Bible is 'inspired by God' (2 Timothy 3:16) and what we mean by the authority of scripture. I often think that what people do with the Bible is far more important than what they say they believe about it, and one of the features of mainstream Christianity throughout its history has been the centrality of reading the Bible and allowing ourselves to be shaped by it. If we need convincing that this is really important, then all we need to consider is this: if we want to be disciples of Jesus, the only place we can go to find out about him are the four accounts of his life in the New Testament which we call the gospels.[17] Once we start to read those books, we discover that Jesus and his biographers constantly refer back to the 39 books of the Old Testament, which tell the long and twisting story of God's relationship with the people of Israel, among whom Jesus was born. After that, we will want to know how people put their knowledge of Jesus and his teaching into practice, and for this we will want to read the other 23 books of the New Testament.

Hopefully that all seems perfectly logical, yet still many Christians do not read the Bible outside church. Some don't seem to feel it's that important, but hopefully if you're reading a book like this you won't need a lot of convincing. More likely the problem is that the Bible is a large and complicated book and you're either not sure how to make sense of what is happening, or else you know that people disagree about how to interpret the Bible and simply feel confused about what to make of what you read. Don't worry; help is at hand. Interpretation is not as hard as you might think. Remember that just because something is in the Bible it does not mean that it's an example to be followed. The problem many people have with the Old Testament is that there are lots of examples of people doing horrific things, sometimes in the name of God, or following laws and customs which seem very strange and foreign to many of us. The clue to understanding is in the title: 'Old' Testament. This part of the Bible prepares the way for Jesus, who, we find, then proceeds to declare that some of it is no longer in operation and that other parts need to be understood in a new way. As a very simple rule of thumb, if being a disciple is about following Jesus, then if something in the Old Testament doesn't look like the kind of thing Jesus would do, then don't do it![18] I know that is a massive oversimplification, and that God speaks through the whole Bible, not just the New Testament, but I hope that helps you to see that there is a method to interpreting the Bible and it isn't just a matter of conflicting opinions.

So how do we read the Bible in a way that helps us to connect more deeply with God and connect God with the whole of life?

To start with, you need a translation of the Bible that you find easy to read. The Authorised King James Version is a classic of the English language, but very few of us read 17th-century English in our day-to-day lives![19] Translation always involves balancing literal accuracy with ease of reading. Modern Bible versions such as the New Revised Standard Version (NRSV) or the New International Version (NIV) are regarded as being strong on accuracy, whereas the New Century Version (NCV), the New Living Translation (NLT) and The Message (MSG) are easy to read but sacrifice some accuracy on the way. Be aware of the differences, but find what works for you.

Far too many people have tried to read the Bible from the first page to the last and given up only a few books in. It really helps to know a bit of background to what you're reading and to have some explanations as you go. Fortunately, there is a wealth of resources to help you do this, available in a variety of media and online. Bible reading notes, such as those produced by the BRF and Scripture Union, provide a systematic reading scheme to get you gradually through the whole of the Bible by giving you a passage to read, explanation where necessary, some things to think about and some suggestions for prayer. When you want to go a bit deeper, there are various schemes available to help you read the whole of the Bible in one year. Top biblical scholarship is also made easily accessible to ordinary readers in the complete Old and New Testament commentary series by John Goldingay and Tom Wright.[20] Every passage is illustrated by a story and then explained in its original context with hints of what it means for us. I can't recommend these books enough!

Studying the Bible is just one way of allowing it to shape us. In recent years, there has been a huge rediscovery of various ways of meditating using the Bible, in order to allow it to sink in more deeply, and to allow God to speak to us as we allow scripture to shape our imagination. One popular method is called *lectio divina*, or 'divine reading'. Take a short passage of scripture and first read it over several times to make sure you understand the words. Next, spend some time meditating on it. In the Old Testament, the word 'meditation' literally means 'murmuring', repeating words of scripture over and over again to reflect deeply on the meaning of each one of them. A good way to do this is to take a single verse of the Bible and think deeply about the full meaning and significance of each word at a time. The third stage is to pray in response to what you feel God has been saying through your meditation. The final stage is contemplation, simply sitting in silence, knowing that through this process you have been engaging with God, who is with you.

Another popular method is known as 'Ignatian' reading, after the 16th-century spiritual leader St Ignatius of Loyola. The Ignatian approach works best with gospel stories, although it could be used in other passages. First, read the passage several times over to become really familiar with what is going on. The main part is then to let your imagination and senses go to work. Try to put yourself into the story, either as a character or as a spectator. What do you see, hear, touch, smell and taste? As you play out the biblical story in your imagination, at some point you are going to arrive close to Jesus. What do you want to say to him? (Loyola originally encouraged people to ask a question, but there might be something else you want to say.) Finally, what do you imagine Jesus saying to you in reply? Some people find this last part quite worrying, in case we imagine something that is wrong or misleading, but since our meditation has been guided by scripture all the way, we can trust the Holy Spirit not to let us down now, though as always we should 'test everything' and 'hold fast to what is good' (1 Thessalonians 5:21).

As you can see, there are lots of different ways to read and engage with the Bible, but in the end the most important thing is to read it. I have a postgraduate degree in New Testament studies but that's not the reason why I know the Bible fairly well. When I became a Christian in my teens, one of the first things I was told was to try to read a little of the Bible every day. What I know now beyond any shadow of a doubt is that if you do that, it becomes a habit and over time it shapes your thinking in ways you would never have imagined at the start. You get to know the Bible by simply reading it.

2 Creation

For all that we cannot truly know and follow Jesus without the Bible, the scriptures themselves tell us that they are not the only source of knowledge about God. The Irish missionary Columbanus, one of the greatest teachers among the Celtic Christians, spoke of there being two books, the book of scripture and the book of creation. 'If you wish to know the creator,' Columbanus said, 'come to know his creatures.'[21] This should come as no surprise when we remember the number of times Jesus turned to the natural world around him to illustrate an aspect of the kingdom of God. Paul speaks of how God's 'eternal power and divine nature… have been understood and seen through the things he has made' (Romans 1:20), echoing the Old Testament understanding that God's glory and wisdom are reflected in his creation (e.g. Psalm 19:1–4 or Job 12:7–8).

Some of us respond instinctively to the presence of God in creation, but for others of us, perhaps as a result of our education, which tells us that the natural world is simply a set of impersonal processes, reading the book of creation is something that we need to relearn. Again, there are resources we can draw on to help us,[22] but the most important thing is to tear ourselves away from our desks and screens, go outside and… just stand there.

I love the outdoors, but I'm not always too good at consciously sensing God there. During a retreat on the Holy Island of Lindisfarne, I asked my friend Ray Simpson, founder of our Community, what he could suggest to help me connect better with God in creation. Ray immediately pointed to Jesus' invitation to think about how God clothes the grass of the field (Matthew 6:30) and suggested I went off and spent some time looking at grass! I went somewhere quiet and spent half an hour simply staring at the grass on which I was sitting (you can imagine why I didn't want anyone to see me). We take grass for granted, just a mass of green. I started looking at individual blades and, as the minutes ticked by, I started to realise God was speaking to me. Apparently, there can be over 50,000 blades of grass in one square metre of ground, and yet Jesus claimed God is aware of, and clothes, all of them. I came to that retreat worried and anxious. God reminded me that if he could keep in his mind all that grass, he could definitely hold on to my problems too. For weeks afterwards, the sight of grass made me secretly smile, as it brought that vital reminder back to me.

3 Life experiences

The third way we learn is through our life experiences and, often intertwined with them, from other people. As we will see in the next chapter, it is vital to see our life as a journey, and, as I know from navigating in the mountains, it is essential to stop regularly and take stock of where you are. Often it's only when we are overtaken by some kind of personal crisis that we're forced to start thinking about how what happens to us, and how we respond to it, shapes the people we have become.

Likewise, we can always learn from other people. One of the most help-ful pieces of guidance I ever read was to 'let the best argument win', no matter who was saying it. If it's right, it's right. Similarly, I think it's good in any situation to regard the person who knows the most about something as the expert and to listen to them. It sounds obvious, but it's so easy not to do it. We can also learn from unhelpful, hostile and negative people. Any conflict is worth reflecting on. Can we see the other person's point of view? Is there a grain of truth in any of their criticisms of us? Those of us who are highly self-critical also need friends who can remind us of the positives about ourselves.

4 Other Christians, past and present

Earlier I mentioned the Irish saint Columbanus. There is much to learn from our spiritual ancestors across the centuries if we will take the trouble to find out about them. It broadens our minds to see that there are other ways of living out Christian faith than just the ones we know. It inspires us to see how God often uses ordinary people to do sometimes quite extraordinary things. It can also be really helpful to see how others struggled with being a Christian. Churches are not always easy places to be. In the seventh century, the Celtic Christians were forced to come into closer conformity with the ways of the wider church. They were not happy. The community at Lindisfarne was now led by Bishop Cuthbert, who in earlier life had been a shepherd, an athlete, a pastor, an evangelist and a hermit. Cuthbert was rooted in the Celtic ways but committed to unity, even if it was painful. As he tried to persuade other members of the community to be reconciled to this, there were arguments in their meetings on an almost daily basis. When things got too heated, Cuthbert would simply stand up, smile at everyone and leave the room, ending the meeting. He did that every day until some sort of calm was restored. I wish I was more like that, but reading about people like Cuthbert reminds me that with God's help I can be.

5 Imagination

When you read the letters of Paul in the New Testament, you might like to notice how often he refers to the importance of the mind (e.g. Romans 12:2). What we think determines a large part of what we feel and how we act. Medical evidence seems to suggest that the more active our minds are when we are younger, the sharper they will remain when we get older. Since 'the earth is the Lord's and all that is in it' (Psalm 24:1), all truth is God's truth, and all knowledge and learning are part of our enjoyment and exploration of God's creation. This, if you ever needed it, is the theological basis for trainspotting! I'm not poking fun at railway (or plane or bus) enthusiasts, but making the serious point that whatever exercises our mind in a creative and expanding way is a good thing. Thinking people are growing people. Intelligence and educational achievement are not the same thing. Learning how to plant potatoes or build a cupboard is just as life-giving as learning about Renaissance art or modern sculpture.

Be a lifelong learner through scripture, creation, experience, other people past and present, and in whatever catches your imagination!

To think about:

- When has the Bible shaped what you have thought or done, and how did it do that?

- 'All truth is God's truth.' Could gaining a new area of knowledge or a new skill be lifegiving for you right now?

For a group:

- Share how you read your Bible – what works for you, what you find difficult and how your different approaches might help each other.

4

Waymark two:
journey with a Soul Friend

We regard the Christian life as a journey and, like Paul, we 'press on towards the goal… of the heavenly call of God in Christ Jesus' (Philippians 3:14). We meet with our Soul Friend at least three times a year to share with them the progress we are making or the difficulties we are facing. They help us to discern what God is doing in our lives at the present time and where he might be leading us. Our Soul Friend is not, however, expected to act as our pastor, counsellor, spiritual director or confessor, unless we choose to seek out a person who has those specific gifts.

We regard two particular practices as important in helping us on our journey with God.

Regular retreats: a retreat is an opportunity for quiet and reflection with God. Individual circumstances and lifestyles mean that this will be worked out in different ways, but it is vital that we take such time regularly. This may take the form of a designated 'quiet day', or we may only be able to set aside a period of a few hours. An annual retreat away from home is encouraged if at all possible.

Pilgrimage: the Bible is full of people making journeys. The Celtic missionaries to Britain were adventurous travellers. Pilgrimage is about visiting significant places and seeking new experiences that will stimulate and inspire us on our journey with God. We visit, reflect and pray at places that are part of our spiritual heritage, such as Lindisfarne and Iona, and places which have become significant to our own spiritual history. When we are able to, we take these opportunities to travel as an outward reminder that God is always on the move and we are called to follow where he leads us.

Life as a journey is an image with which everyone is familiar. When a football team enters the first round of the FA Cup, the journalists write that they are 'on the road to Wembley'. When celebrities learn to dance on Saturday-night TV they do interviews about their 'Amazing *Strictly* journey!' It's no surprise, then, to find that the Bible is full of stories of people on journeys, and that journeying itself is an image of our relationship with God.

That said, Christianity is also irreducibly something we do together and, on this journey with God, no one should travel alone. We have seen already the importance of meeting with other Christians in small groups, but also that for many of us this is practically very difficult. Alison Morgan acknowledges this when she writes that 'the challenge is finding ways, in our time-stressed world, to actually carve out time and space to be truly known, deeply loved and radically challenged to follow Christ with our entire lives'.[23] Tony Pullen, in his much-acclaimed book on discipleship, goes further: 'If I am to be truly discipled… I will need to be open with someone who can help me to grow into the image of Jesus.'[24] At this point, many of us will feel some questions rising up. Why would I want to be open with someone else – after all, most of us have plenty of things we'd rather keep hidden! Secondly, even if I wanted something like this, where would I find it?

The answer is to be found in a practice of the Celtic and desert Christians, which they regarded as nothing less than essential and which most of the church has forgotten for over 1,500 years. In Irish it's called an *anam chara*, which translates directly into English as a 'Soul Friend'. Here is how our Way of Life defines it:

> The early church in these islands and elsewhere practised the ministry of 'Soul Friendship'. A Soul Friend is a mature Christian who is in sympathy with our Way of Life, and who helps us to discern and respond appropriately to God's will, grow in maturity, responsibility and wholeness, and to deepen our relationship with God. Our Soul Friend helps us to work out our personal application of the Way of Life, reviews it with us at regular intervals, and is a companion to us on our spiritual journey.

In *Creating Community*, I devoted a whole chapter to explaining how this practice developed, and also how it can be seen in the ministries of Jesus and Paul. But why is it so important? One-to-one relationships have always been important in Christian discipleship. In the 17th century, Richard Baxter, the minister of Kidderminster, wrote a book called *The Reformed Pastor*, which became a classic of Christian ministry. Baxter visited every family in his parish to talk to them personally about their faith and saw many people come to life in a new way in their relationship with God.

When I was in a university Christian Union, it was normal practice that, if a person became a Christian, someone would meet weekly with them to help them read the Bible and pray. In the 1980s, some new churches became very directive through these kinds of one-to-one relationships to the extent that what became known as 'heavy shepherding' is still seen as an abuse of pastoral care and, as far as I can tell, for most Christians the idea of being voluntarily 'accountable' to someone else is not attractive. It's not hard to see why. If I ask any audience whether they would like to be accountable to another Christian, nearly everyone finds something to look at on the floor or the ceiling, and the few brave ones who keep eye contact indicate a very clear no! But if I ask whether anyone thinks it might be good, every few months, to meet for an hour or so with someone who is solely there to listen to them, encourage them and pray for them, a lot of people suddenly start to look interested. That is what Soul Friendship is all about. I now see about a dozen people individually every couple of months. (We're a small church, so that is a significant proportion.) We talk about prayer, the Bible, families, jobs, managing time and having fun! Outside of our Sunday gatherings, it is the most important thing I do. I come without an agenda, listen and see where God takes our conversation. What I see is people growing – connecting more deeply with God and, just as importantly, making the connections between God and the rest of their life. In a later chapter, I will explain how to find a Soul Friend. Small groups are great for many people, but the Celtic Christians were emphatic that Soul Friendship is for everyone. 'A person without a Soul Friend,' St Brigid said, 'is like a body without a head.'

Every journey needs breaks. In the mountains it's always wise, especially in bad weather, to keep checking the map or to take a new compass bearing. You also need to stop in order to eat and drink and catch your breath. Life is no different, and yet the world we live in urges us to be in touch 24 hours a day and to pack ever more in – even though we're working ever longer hours. It is no surprise that stress and other related health problems are epidemic. Jesus was a very busy person, but you never get the impression that he was in a hurry. You also see him deliberately walking away from the demands of the crowd in order to rest and spend time seeking God.

The only way to make sure this happens is to plan it, and like most things it's best to start small and work upwards. My friend David Cole (Brother Cassian), in one of the best short introductions to Christian meditation and contemplative prayer, suggests that we learn to 'meditate momentarily' for a few seconds, 'divert daily' for ten to twenty minutes, 'withdraw weekly' for a few hours, 'make a date monthly' for a whole day if possible, and 'abdicate annually' from your responsibilities to go away for a few days focussing on God.[25] He gives good practical advice on how to do each of these things. The Retreat Association (**retreats. org.uk**) provides a directory of places where you can go to find some space for a day or longer, as well as lots of helpful advice about how to spend your time.

The final expression of our journey with God is through pilgrimage. Again, this is an ancient idea, which is suddenly becoming popular again. Every year, thousands of people walk the Camino, the pilgrim route to Santiago de Compostela in Spain. Others will walk the 103 kilometres of the St Cuthbert's Way from Melrose in Scotland to the island of Lindisfarne, some of them walking barefoot across the sands following the iconic posts that lead to Holy Island. Others make their way to the shrine of Mary at Walsingham, or go to join the ecumenical worship at Taizé in France. All over Europe, pilgrimage routes are being marked out for people who want to step away from their daily routine for what may be a once-in-a-lifetime adventure.

Many of us will have at least heard about Geoffrey Chaucer's rag-tag collection of medieval pilgrims depicted in *The Canterbury Tales*. In those days, pilgrimage was about making a special effort to try to earn merit with God and reduce the time spent in purgatory on the way to heaven. Modern pilgrimage is about making a symbolic journey, which brings into focus our inner journey with God and sets aside time in the hope of meeting him in a special way along the route. Many Christians already do this every year, without ever thinking of it as pilgrimage. Thousands gather at Easter for Spring Harvest, and thousands more at summer festivals like New Wine, Soul Survivor or the Keswick Convention. Yet this is pilgrimage, time set aside for God that involves travelling to a new location. In some ways these festivals might be seen as pop-up pilgrimages, creating for a week a special setting for a meeting with God. Certainly, for those who go, and return year after year uplifted by the experience, the fields of tents do have the same quality as a permanent shrine.

For reasons of health, mobility, family or money, not everyone is able to go on pilgrimage, even if they want to. Nevertheless, we can still access the benefits of it from our own home. Part of our time of personal reflection, done in the spaces we have carved out in our regular retreat times, however long or short they are, might be to reflect on the shape of our own journey with God. We might start to draw up a timeline, looking at the shape of our life and marking where God has been significantly active – or absent – along the way, reflecting on what contributed to this and what we might learn from it. Knowing where we have come from feeds into a fresh understanding of where we are now, and inevitably into seeking God to map out the future. For more ideas on how you can be a pilgrim without leaving home, I can only recommend a recent book by Richard Littledale which does precisely that, as he invites us to reflect on what leaving home, taking provisions, making communications, finding companions, coping with distractions and coming to our journey's end mean in our day-to-day lives.[26]

As part of my own living out of this Way of Life, I try to visit one place connected in some way with Celtic spirituality every year. I have discovered that these small-scale journeys of discovery can lead to unusual encounters with the God of surprises. In 2013 I had a sabbatical, which I entered utterly exhausted, not least from all the extra work of having to make sure everything kept running while I was off for two months. The only thing I had definitely planned was to walk the Celtic-inspired St Cuthbert's Way. I wanted to make it a more immersive experience so, rather than sleep in bed and breakfast accommodation, I decided that I would try to backpack it and camp. I soon realised what I was taking on. The walk normally lasts four days, but having to divert to campsites added to each day's distance. On the first day I walked 31 kilometres carrying not only my day kit but also a tent and camping gear. It was also a heatwave and during the day I drank nearly six litres of water.

In the mid-afternoon I was between two villages in the Scottish Borders, out of water and still with a third of the distance to travel. Ahead was a small village and I realised I would have no option but to bang on doors like a beggar and hope that someone would give me a drink. Feeling dehydrated and dejected, I muttered a prayer: 'Lord, some of that daily bread stuff – you know, basic needs – would be really helpful right now.' As I trudged up a small but unwelcome hill, I saw a woman come out and stand right in the middle of the road. As I approached she called out, 'Are you the person backpacking the St Cuthbert's Way?' 'Yes,' I said, 'how on earth did you know?' 'You met my husband an hour ago. He's walking part of it too and phoned on to say you were coming.' With that, she offered me a cup of tea and some cake. For half an unreal moment I felt like a modern version of Elijah and the ministering angel (1 Kings 19:4–9), who also turned up unexpectedly and offered cake! 'Thank you,' I said, 'but I really urgently just need to get some water.' With that I looked across the street and there in front of me attached to a wall was a tap with drinking water!

When I got to the campsite my feet were blistered to destruction and, although I tried to soldier on for another day, I ended up having to abandon my pilgrimage and take the bus to Lindisfarne. But it didn't matter. Even in that one day, what I had come for had been achieved. I needed to meet God in a fresh way and that is exactly what happened. Going out into the fields and tracks, carrying all I needed on my back and leaving normal civilisation behind, reminded me of the essentials of life – food, water and the kindness of strangers. God also reminded me that he really can give us daily bread when we ask him. As I look back to that day, when I turned the corner of the street, I also turned a corner in my relationship with God. My praying was refreshed and renewed that day. 'Live deliberately' is the motto of a friend of mine. Pilgrimage, retreat and the help of a Soul Friend are all reminders to do that in a conscious awareness that our lives really are a journey with God.

To think about:

- Who do you have who you regard as a companion on your journey with God?

- How do you build space to reflect into your life?

For a group:

- What could we do together to become more aware of what is happening in each others' lives in a way that is supportive?

5

Waymark three:
keep a rhythm of prayer,
work and recreation

Prayer

The life of Jesus was fuelled by prayer and he taught the need to pray always (Luke 18:1). We commit ourselves to a regular pattern of daily prayer, alone or with others. Ways of praying will vary according to our personality, but we affirm and encourage every kind of prayer from silent contemplation to celebratory praise. Set forms of prayer can be provided, as can guidance about how to establish and deepen our personal prayer life.

Work

Jesus spoke frequently about work (e.g. Luke 12:42–43). God intended from the beginning that human beings should engage in beneficial work (Genesis 2:15). We therefore welcome work as a gift from God and seek to engage in it, whether through paid employment, the necessary tasks of daily life or other constructive activities. Work involving values or practices which conflict with our Way of Life should be avoided as much as possible, but we seek the presence of God in every task, even unattractive ones. If we are unemployed or unclear what our work should be, we seek advice and guidance. We seek to resist pressures to overwork because it misuses time which should rightfully be given to God, others or ourselves.

Recreation
Jesus taught that 'the sabbath was made for humankind' (Mark 2:27) because God himself rested at the end of creation (Genesis 2:1–3). In the Old Testament, even the land had a sabbath rest every seventh year (Leviticus 25:1–4). Since time spent in rest and recreation is as essential as time spent in prayer and work, we build regular time for restoration and renewal of body, mind and spirit into our personal Way of Life.

Prayer

If I could only ever teach people one thing about how to live as a Christian, I would try to teach them how to pray more easily. This isn't because I think that I'm some kind of expert on prayer. I'm absolutely not. In fact, I've often said that if I wrote a book on prayer it would be called *God, what on earth are you doing?* (Actually, it would be called something less polite than that and then no one would ever publish it!) Nevertheless, prayer is the very core of our connection with God. It is to the spirit what breathing is to the body. Yet it's also my observation that the majority of Christians find prayer much harder than they need to, and often live with a draining feeling that, however they are managing to pray, it isn't good enough.

This Way of Life draws on two insights which I hope will free us in our practice and experience of prayer. The first is the importance of seeing prayer as a rhythm. The second is the startling realisation that the way that people prayed in the Bible is rather different from the way that many of us are taught to pray today.

Rhythms are an integral part of creation. There is the rhythm of morning and night, the rhythm of the seasons and the rhythm of the tides. In our bodies, there is the rhythm of sleeping and waking, the rhythm of breathing and the rhythm of our heartbeats. Prayer, as it is practised in the Bible, aligns itself with these rhythms. Many of us have been either challenged or depressed by Paul's encouragement to 'pray without ceasing' (1 Thessalonians 5:17). Monastic spirituality has found various ways of using techniques of meditative prayer which can actually make this a reality, but it's worth taking a step back to think about prayer as Paul experienced and practised it. Remember that in the ancient world people did not have watches, so they used the big clock in the sky. Unless you could afford lots of candles, you woke up when it got light and went to bed when it got dark. It was therefore natural to mark both ends of the day in prayer, exactly as Psalm 92 celebrates: 'It is good to give thanks to the Lord, to sing praises to your name, O Most High; to declare your steadfast love in the morning, and your faithfulness by night.' Devout Jews like Daniel prayed three times a day (Daniel 6:10), and the very devoted author of Psalm 119 prayed seven times a day (v. 164).

Once we realise that this was how Jews prayed, we can see it in the New Testament even though the authors do not draw attention to it because they simply take it for granted. Like all other Jews, Jesus prays early in the morning every day (Mark 1:35); it's just that sometimes he started even earlier. Likewise, he prays every evening (Matthew 14:23); it's just that sometimes he goes away alone to do it and unusual things happen. We can be pretty certain that Paul, being a devout Jew before he was a devout Christian, also followed this daily rhythm of prayer. When he tells the Thessalonians that he prays for them night and day (1 Thessalonians 3:10), he is not drawing attention to how often he prays but to the fact that every time he prays, he prays for them.

Most of us will have been taught that we ought to try to pray every day. For many of us this means trying to find a time to pray, and then either feeling bad if we miss it, or struggling with the distractions that crowd our mind when we do stop to pray. It takes so much of that pressure off if we can grasp that we don't have to pray for a long time if we don't go for a long time without praying! I was talking to someone recently who was distressed by the fact that she could not spend half an hour in prayer and meditation every morning. Knowing something of her domestic circumstances, I pointed out to her that she would be lucky to manage that any day of the week, and that ten minutes, if that was all she had, was fine. One of the most liberating insights into prayer I have ever heard is this: 'to reach for God is to reach God'.[27] Ultimately, prayer is not about what we can do, but about opening ourselves up to what God can do. Paul never wrote a truer word than when he said, 'We do not know how to pray as we ought,' but in the same breath he writes that 'the Spirit helps us in our weakness' and intercedes for us (Romans 8:26–27). That means the most important thing we can do in prayer is simply to show up. The very intention of trying to pray is all that the Holy Spirit needs in order to capture and present to God our needs, desires and longings more clearly than our words ever could. If we can check in regularly with God throughout the day, even if it is only for a few minutes at a time, we will find our prayer life growing and our sensitivity to the Spirit increasing. Obviously, it's good to learn how to pray for more extended periods of time, but the wisdom of the centuries shows that little and often is the foundation for it all.

The first insight concerns when we pray. The second is about how we pray. Many of us will have been taught that prayer is simply 'talking to God', which is a good place to start, but many of us seem to have difficulty doing that. I hear things like, 'I'd like to pray for longer, but I just run out of things to say', or 'I don't want my prayers to just be a list, but I'm not sure what else to do', or 'I'm not sure you can really pray about some things'. Knowing how to talk to God is harder than it seems. I remember in my late teens having a significant encounter with the Holy Spirit, which left me wanting to experience more of God's power in my life. One of my friends gave me a little booklet full of Bible verses and a challenge to spend an hour a day praising God because this would bring wonderful benefits. As I still lived with my parents, I reckoned the only way to do this would be to wake up early, so I set my alarm, struggled to open my eyes, got out the booklet and for an hour I read every verse and tried to add to them prayers of my own. I can't remember how many days I managed to do this but it was significantly less than a week! Years later, as an ordained church minister, I again found myself struggling for words as the busyness and responsibility of doing 'God stuff' all day left my mind tired and distracted whenever I tried to pray. That was the point at which I discovered that simply trying to talk to God in my own words was not the way that Jews and Christians originally prayed.

Scholars tell us that Jewish prayer grew out of their fundamental declaration of faith: 'Hear, O Israel: the Lord is our God, the Lord alone' (Deuteronomy 6:4). Those words are known as the *Shema*, from the Hebrew command to 'hear'. It became a custom not only to declare these words at the beginning and end of the day, but also to add prayers of thanksgiving, and then prayers of petition. This is almost certainly what the writer of Daniel imagines his hero doing, and how Jesus and Paul would have prayed. The psalms also became part of these daily prayers. There is therefore nothing inauthentic or second best about praying using other people's words, especially when they are the words of scripture. I'm an Anglican, so you might expect me to say this, but it is honestly my experience that having set forms of prayer, especially ones that are so simple they can be memorised, gives people something to say which enables them to open their mouths in prayer and, as they begin to connect with God using these prepared words, it gives them the freedom and confidence to begin those personal conversations with God which they always wanted to have but weren't sure how. There are varieties of daily prayer books available and also lots of good phone apps as well.[28] It's actually never been easier to pray![29]

In a later chapter on listening to God, I will say something about Christian meditation and contemplative prayer, but of course there is probably no limit to the ways in which we can reach for God and reach God. The most important thing is simply to start your own daily rhythm of prayer, talk about it with your Soul Friend, if you need help, then just keep going (no matter what) and see what happens.

Work

Proverbially, no one ever looked back on their life and said, 'I wish I'd spent more time at the office.' Lotteries and competitions offer us more money than we could ever imagine, with the promise that if you win you'll never have to work again. So often we regard work as a curse when actually the Bible says it is a blessing. When I lived in a town in the north-west of England during a recession, I saw first-hand the misery of unemployment, when a young man asked for prayer before a job interview on Monday. It was for simple work as a painter and decorator but he was one of 59 people who turned up. My city is full of migrants who have come from all over the world in search of a decent job to provide a better future for their family.

Work is a gift from God. In the first creation story, the two humans are told to 'fill the earth and subdue it' (Genesis 1:28). In the next chapter, we will explore what this does and does not mean. There is however genuine truth in the old joke about the vicar cycling through a country village who stopped to watch one of his parishioners digging a flower bed. 'Isn't it wonderful how the Lord created your garden,' he said piously. 'I'm sure it is,' said the man digging, 'but you should have seen the state of it when he had it to himself.' Quite simply, the creation tells us that the earth is incomplete without what human beings do with it, and therefore human beings cannot reach their potential unless they work.

The problem for many of us is that our experience of work is nothing like that. This is a consequence of living in a fallen world that no longer conforms to God's original purposes for it. In the story we call the 'fall,' where human beings break their relationship with God, they are told that as a consequence their lives will be characterised by toil and sweat (Genesis 3:17–19). This is where it is vital to remember that discipleship is about being part of God's rescue plan for all creation and for us personally, and about connecting God with the whole of life.

Our attitude to our work is a good place to start. A very helpful question to ask ourselves is to what extent we live to work or work to live. In other words, is our work the most important part of our life, something that we do as an end in itself? Or is work simply the way in which we earn money in order to support something which is more important to us, whether that is providing for our family, or meeting our basic needs so that we can concentrate on something else we really care about outside of paid work? It is much easier to cope with unfulfilling work if we know that it is simply the means to an end of doing what does fulfil us. If we have a career, it is important to understand what our values are within it. A member of my church holds a senior position in a large international company. The job is well paid and uses all of her educational and professional skills. For several years, we have talked and prayed about whether she should move jobs. The issue is not money, but of feeling valued for what she does. She knows that if she is going to give her best, she has to be in a setting where others want the best for her. Anything less would be unfulfilling. She has now found a new job.

Work does not have to be paid. It can be voluntary, family, or doing something creative. I also greatly admire a friend who is blind and cannot find work, yet he refuses to lie in bed all day and gets up as if he was going to work. That allows him to do something constructive with each day, which in his case means using his computer to read books and develop his very active and enquiring mind. The first Bible verse I ever memorised was Colossians 3:23 (NEB): 'Whatever you are doing, put your whole heart into it, as if you were doing it for the Lord.'

Recreation

If we are called to work, we are also called to rest. The creation story ends with God resting on the seventh day and blessing and setting that day apart (Genesis 2:1–3), and Jesus was clear that this sabbath day was intended as a gift and blessing for us (Mark 2:27). This reminds us on the one hand that how we use the time of rest is not meant to be governed by legalistic rules. It's worth remembering that many of the early Christians were household slaves who would not have been able to take a day off unless their owners gave permission. Christians of an older generation may remember grim 'sabbaths' of compulsory churchgoing and prohibition of toys and games. On a holiday in a very strict part of Scotland we once saw the gates of the village playground chained shut on the sabbath to stop any unfortunate child from sinning! This is hardly encouraging a joyful celebration of God's good creation.

On the other hand, the biggest problem many of us have is in taking enough rest time at all. In Britain, we work some of the longest hours in Europe and there is repeated pressure to deregulate the limits placed on how long people can be expected to work. The result of this is an epidemic of stress-related illnesses, both physical and mental. The prevalence of smartphones, laptops and the more recent work from home culture, ushered in due to the pandemic, have all led to increased pressure on employees never to switch off their devices and work above and beyond contracted hours.

I learned a long time ago that if you do not take control of your own time then someone else will. I am fortunate in having a job in which I can take a full day off every week (though technically there are no other time limits on when I am available). You may not be able to do that, but what is absolutely vital is to build into every week time when you do something that for you is renewing and restorative. It doesn't matter what that is, as long as it is something different from your regular occupation. I often say, 'If it doesn't have a diary date it doesn't exist,' so put these times into your weekly calendar because it will stop the time being stolen by something, or someone, else. We must also remember that our bodies themselves are a gift from God and take proper care of them. Again, exercise varies from person to person. If you're very unfit, then simply going for a five-minute walk will literally be a step forward. For others, it will be a gym session several times a week. The important thing to remember is that this is all part of tuning in to the God-given rhythms of life, which help us to live in harmony with our creator.

To think about:

- What does your daily or weekly rhythm of prayer look like (and what changes might you want to make to it)?

- To what extent do you live to work (whether paid or other responsibilities) or work in order to live (doing the things you feel are most important)?

For a group:

- What could we plan to do together that is simply fun?

6

Waymark four:
live as simply as possible

Jesus said, 'You cannot serve God and wealth… For where your treasure is, there your heart will be also' (Matthew 6:24, 21). He also encouraged us to trust that God will always give us our daily bread (Matthew 6:11). We seek to be open and accountable before God (and, if appropriate, our Soul Friend) for the way we use our money and possessions, handle our time and activities, and the quality of our relationships and hospitality. We are conscious that we are stewards, not owners, of these things, and we are ready to make them and ourselves available to others as God guides us.

Faced with global poverty and environmental crisis, we seek to 'live simply that others may simply live'. This will mean different things for different people, and we do not judge one another. We also enjoy and celebrate the good things God gives us and understand that there is a time to feast as well as to fast. We seek to order our possessions, activities and relationships in a way which frees us to be fully attentive to God, others and ourselves, and we seek to get rid of those things which overload or clutter our lives. Our clothing and surroundings should reflect our God-given individuality, expressing beauty while rejecting extravagance. We also stand against the

*spirit of materialism by practising hospitality wherever possible
and by committing to proportionate and generous financial giving.*

Worship

The purpose of our Way of Life is to enable us to connect more deeply
with God and to connect God with the whole of life. In his letter to
the Christians in Rome, Paul spends eleven chapters explaining how,
through the death and resurrection of Jesus, God has been faithful
to his promise and purpose to redeem human beings and to set all
creation free from its captivity to decay and death. He ends with an
explosion of praise and thanksgiving: 'O the depth of the riches and
wisdom and knowledge of God!… To him be the glory for ever. Amen'
(Romans 11:33, 36). That sounds like he's about to sign off, but in fact
he just pauses for breath and then writes this: 'I appeal to you therefore,
brothers and sisters, by the mercies of God, to present your bodies as
a living sacrifice, holy and acceptable to God, which is your spiritual
worship. Do not be conformed to this world, but be transformed by
the renewing of your minds, so that you may discern what is the will
of God – what is good and acceptable and perfect' (Romans 12:1–2).
Worship, therefore, is the offering of our whole lives to God as we live
them in harmony with him. What we do when we come together with
other Christians, important as that is, is just taking a regular opportunity to put that into words.

When God had finished creating all material things he declared them
to be good, and creation still declares the glory of God (e.g. Psalm
19:1). Yet the whole material world, just like human beings, is also
infected by the effects of sin, and unless our minds are continually
being renewed, as Paul says, we will find ourselves committing the
ultimate sin, which is to have 'exchanged the truth about God for a
lie and worshipped and served the creature, rather than the Creator'
(Romans 1:25). Paul is drawing on what the Old Testament says about
idolatry, which is more than just worshipping other gods, but placing
anything other than God in the place of highest honour. That is why

Jesus said we cannot serve two masters, and why our use of money and possessions is an indicator of the quality of our relationship with God just as much as our praying.

Money

The Bible does not say that money is the root of all evil. What it actually says is that 'the love of money is a root of all kinds of evil' (1 Timothy 6:10). Money, as the old proverb says, is a good servant but a bad master. It seems to me that two things hinder the work of the kingdom of God in today's world more than any other: a shortage of willing people and a shortage of money. The Bible never says that there is anything wrong with making money, but its focus is on what we do with it. In 2014, the BBC ran a short series called *Digby Jones: The new trouble-shooter* in which this experienced business leader and independent member of the House of Lords went into small businesses to help them to grow. He explained at the start that he loved small businesses because 'they provide jobs and their taxes help fund the schools and hospitals we all use'. That seems to me to sum up a Christian vision for economics and society, where our personal well-being is bound up with the good of all. As John Wesley's teaching is often summarised: make all you can, save all you can, give all you can.

Money is high on the agenda in today's churches. In some places, it is at the top of the agenda in a desperate desire to maintain ancient buildings or fund full-time ministers, but in others crowds flock in to listen to the so-called prosperity gospel that faith in Christ will bring us wealth, health and success in all we do. This teaching is growing and it is wrong for so many reasons. If it were true then nearly everyone in the New Testament church failed, if their lives of suffering and struggle are anything to go by.

So, if making money is good, and saving wisely is encouraged, what does the Bible say about giving? The heart of the Christian message is the unending generosity of God in creating, redeeming and sustaining everything that exists. One of the defining characteristics of a Christian is reflecting that generosity in and through our own lives. Here are some reasons why giving is so important:

- It shows that we really do trust in the God who can 'satisfy every need… according to his riches in glory in Christ Jesus' (Philippians 4:19).
- It breaks the power of money over us – Jesus said we cannot serve God and wealth (Matthew 6:24), so giving some of it away shows it does not control us.
- It meets the needs of others – 'Open your hand to the poor and needy neighbour in your land' (Deuteronomy 15:11).
- It resources the ministry and mission of the church – '"The labourer deserves to be paid"… especially those who labour in preaching and teaching' (1 Timothy 5:18, 17).
- It's a way of offering worship to God – King David said, 'I will not sacrifice to the Lord my God offerings that cost me nothing' (2 Samuel 24:24, NIV).

Above all, it imitates Jesus, whom we are called to follow – 'For you know the generous act of our Lord Jesus Christ, that though he was rich, yet for your sakes he became poor, so that by his poverty you might become rich' (2 Corinthians 8:9).

I respect those who teach tithing (giving away ten per cent of our income), but I think that ultimately it is an Old Testament tax, which is not taught in the New Testament. Instead, Jesus and Paul urge extravagant generosity. Giving away ten per cent is a good target, but for some of us that is just the beginning. The most important thing, if you do not already do this, is to add up your income, and then start to give away a percentage of it. Supporting the church or a Christian group to which you belong is a very good use of that giving because, in most cases, our giving is their main source of income.

Possessions

Perhaps this is a good moment to say that, in working out our personal application of this Way of Life, one size does not fit all, and it is vital that we do not judge one another. For some people, a simple lifestyle is expressed by a joyful minimalism in which they do not own anything beyond what is absolutely necessary and try to buy only from second-hand shops. That is one way to respond to God. Another is to follow the principle expressed by the artist William Morris: 'Have nothing in your house that you do not know to be useful, or believe to be beautiful.' That speaks of spending our money only on things which are of real value and knowing why we possess them, and it also gets to the heart of the principle of simple living, that we are not so utterly clogged up and cluttered by possessions that our vision of God is obscured and our capacity to respond to others' needs is obstructed.

Time and activities

'Money is power, but time is life.'[30] Psalm 90 prays, 'Teach us to number our days that we may gain a wise heart' (v. 12), and Paul urges the Ephesians to 'be careful then how you live, not as unwise people but as wise, making the most of the time, because the days are evil' (Ephesians 5:15–16). For many of us, managing money is a challenge, but managing time is even more essential, because even if we are financially comfortable, many of us are time-poor. Our technology enables us to be more in touch than ever before and, as a result, we try to cram ever more into the time that we have. The danger is that we become so taken up with what we are doing next that we no longer live in the present moment. Too often we are physically present with people but mentally absent.

This is where different elements of our Way of Life start to come together. In a later chapter, we will look at the three life-giving principles of simplicity, purity and obedience, which help us to set the overall priorities for our lives. We have already looked at the daily rhythm of prayer, which keeps us connected with God throughout the day, and the rhythms of work and rest, which help us to step out of relentless activity. One of the biggest causes of stress and anxiety is the feeling that we just have too much to do and not enough time to do it in, often worsened by a sense of being pulled apart in different directions. A few years ago, trying to balance the leadership of two churches, an international Christian community and a local neighbourhood organisation, I felt exactly like that. At my annual review, I talked about this and was given some money from a training budget to spend some time with a management consultant. She asked me to think about all the things I was involved in as being like departments in a large company and then to identify how many of them were personally my responsibility. When we worked out that there were 16 and I was responsible for three-quarters of them, we knew the scale of the problem!

Some people retake control of their life by minimising their technology. They use a mobile phone only for emergencies and don't own a computer. Others ration their time online and have times when their phones are turned off. I never look at emails on my day off to keep my head clear, but I love the fact that I can organise so much of my life from a handheld device that fits in my pocket. We're all different. I learned two things from my encounter with overload. The first was that a good system for managing my life was essential.[31] The second is the value of mindfulness or other kinds of meditation to reduce stress and anxiety.[32] Both are vital aids in redeeming my time and helping me more consciously to abide in Jesus (John 15:1–5) rather than submerge in busyness.

Relationships

Simplicity in relationships is rooted in the commandment not to bear false witness towards others (Exodus 20:16). In the sermon on the mount Jesus pushed this further in insisting on plain speaking at all times: 'Let your "Yes" be "Yes", and your "No", "No"' (Matthew 5:37, NKJV), while Paul urged 'speaking the truth in love' (Ephesians 4:15). It has been said that the true test of any kind of community is how it deals with disagreements. Jesus wisely saw this one coming and teaches clearly how to deal with it. First, talk to the other person one-to-one, hoping to resolve the problem. If that fails, get someone else involved. If that fails, then deal with it in a public way (Matthew 18:15–20).

How Christians should behave, with the expression of love as the goal, as described so fully in 1 Corinthians 13, and the establishment of peace (Colossians 3:15) as the guideline, could not be clearer, and yet so many people struggle with this. Often the roots of our anger with others are our own insecurities that we will be diminished if others get away with wronging us, or that we will be further put down by rejection if we confront them, and only a deeper grasp of how much we are loved by God can cure that. It is also made difficult by the fact that we are frequently told to forgive but rarely taught how to do this. 'Forgive and forget' is one of the stupidest things anyone can tell us because we cannot choose to forget. In fact, the Bible never tells us that God forgets anything. Instead, it tells us that sometimes he chooses not to remember (e.g. Isaiah 43:25).

This is how forgiveness works. We acknowledge before God exactly what someone has done to us, not suppressing the tiniest part of the hurt and the hate we feel. (Yes, those are strong words, but so many Christians refuse to believe how angry they really are because they have been told they should not feel that way. Trying to hide our true feelings from an all-knowing, and fortunately all-loving, God does not make much sense if we stop and think about it!) Then we make the choice before God to stop holding the other person's wrongdoing against them. When we think of them, we will deliberately put aside and no longer dwell upon what they have done. We will choose to treat them better than they deserve. If we ask why we should do this, there are three answers. First, we can do this trusting that if justice needs to be done God will take care of it (Romans 12:19). Second, it will make us feel better because now that the poison is out, God can begin healing us inside. Third, and most important, what we are doing for others is precisely what God does for us all the time.

Forgiveness, however, is not the same as reconciliation. Forgiveness is primarily about us and about how we are feeling, which means that we can forgive people who are dead or who are no longer part of our lives. But, without forgiveness, there can be no hope of reconciliation because we will find it almost impossible not to dump anger on those with whom we have disagreed. The most helpful advice I have ever been given about difficult conversations is to think first what actually needs to be said, and then to think about the most sensitive way to say it, which will allow the hearer both to be able to understand what is being said and also to have the best chance to respond in a way that will lead to peace. Only in exceptional circumstances is this not best done one-to-one and in private and preferably face-to-face. Emails and texts are notorious for increasing misunderstanding because it is so hard to read them accurately in the absence of the speaker's tone of voice and the expression on their face.

Hospitality

In the ancient world, the clearest expression of a relationship with a person was whether you were prepared to sit down at a table with them. It is no coincidence that the defining rituals which express coming together as the family of God in both Old and New Testaments involve eating and drinking together. What repeatedly got Jesus into trouble was his deliberate habit of eating with the wrong kinds of people. 'Welcome one another, therefore, just as Christ has welcomed you' (Romans 15:7). Hospitality is a vital expression of a simple lifestyle because it expresses the character and practice of Christ whom we seek to follow, and puts our priorities and possessions into the service of the well-being of other people. The obvious expression of hospitality is welcoming others to eat with us. Sometimes our domestic circumstances, such as a partner with an exhausting job, mean that opening our home is not the easiest way of doing this. A long time ago I was part of a team visiting the Anglican Pro-Cathedral in Brussels. Many of the congregation were frantically busy EU or NATO employees, so the church ministers were paid a lunch allowance to meet them pastorally at the one time they would be free. Buying lunches is how I most often practise hospitality.

But there's an even simpler and more vital form of hospitality, and again it links together different parts of this Way of Life. More than anything else, what many want is just someone to listen to them. To give them that time is a gift, but for the gift not to be empty, we ourselves need to be sufficiently uncluttered in our schedules and in our heads to be free to listen to them. Creating that freedom, to be open to God and open to others, is what the practice of living simply is all about.

To think about:

- How often do you bring before God your financial circumstances and how you use the resources you have?

- Ephesians 4:16 encourages us to make the most of our time, so how do you make sure you do that as much as possible?

For a group:

- Share (as far as you are comfortable) situations involving forgiveness and reconciliation, trying to help each other deal with those that are still unresolved.

7

Waymark five:
celebrate and care for creation

Jesus called himself 'the light of the world [literally, the kosmos]' (John 8:12), and John declares that 'all things came into being through him' (John 1:3). There are many stories of the Celtic saints and other holy people living in harmony with wild creatures. We affirm that God's creation is essentially good, but is corrupted and damaged by the effects of human sin and the influence of the spiritual powers of evil. We believe that creation reveals the glory of God (Psalm 19:1), so we celebrate creation and seek ways to meet with and learn from God through it. We likewise seek to be environmentally aware, living in a way that respects and cares for God's creation and which stands against those values and practices which continue to damage it.

In February 2008 I sat with my back against an easy-angled pile of stones on the summit of Stob a'Choire Odhair (you work out how to pronounce it!) in the Scottish Highlands. It was a clear winter day and unusually there was no wind. In warm clothing, there was no need for me to get down quickly and for 20 minutes I simply gazed at mountains in every direction, capped in white on top and clothed in deep green at their roots in the glens. From nowhere, I felt a deep sense of peace and well-being seeping into me. It's almost impossible to explain this sense of instinctive connection that we have to the natural world, but I've seen it again and again.

The first time I ascended one of the peaks on Skye's magnificently jagged Cuillin ridge, I was walking alone into the rocky upper corrie bowl when I caught up with another solo walker going the same way. We chatted companionably as we climbed, but when the crest of the ridge appeared out of the mist he stopped abruptly, threw out his arms in what looked like an act of worship and shouted in a thick Glaswegian accent, 'Is this not magnificent?'

God's creation has a way of catching up on us like this, whether it's in the wildness of mountains and seas, or the miniature vitality of garden flowers and birds. The 19th-century poet Gerard Manley Hopkins captured the spirituality of creation in 'God's Grandeur': 'The world is charged with the grandeur of God. It will flame out, like shining from shook foil.' Hopkins also evocatively grasps how, in the modern industrial world, we have lost sight of this: 'all is seared with trade; bleared, smeared with toil… the soil is bare now, nor can foot feel, being shod.' Yet, he continues, 'for all this, nature is never spent; there lives the dearest freshness deep down things…'[33] That is precisely what we feel when we reconnect with the natural world, and reconnect we must, before it's too late.

None of this should be a surprise when we look at scripture and lives of Christians down the centuries, but in the wealth of books currently exploring discipleship, there is barely a mention of our relationship to the non-human creation, despite the fact that we are in the middle of an environmental crisis which could have literally catastrophic consequences.

The Bible famously begins in a garden but ends in a city, but even the new Jerusalem of the book of Revelation has 'the river of the water of life, bright as crystal', and 'on either side of the river is the tree of life… and the leaves of the tree are for the healing of the nations' (Revelation 22:1–2). In Genesis the first humans are told to 'fill the earth and subdue it; and have dominion over… every living thing' (Genesis 1:28). This passage has become notorious among some people who see it as Christendom's license to ravage the planet in pursuit of ceaseless economic growth and consumption. It's important to remember that, until the Romantic poets of the late 18th century, most people regarded the wild places of the earth as a terrifying reminder of their human fragility, and never imagined that they could ever be controlled and exploited, let alone destroyed. Furthermore, as we saw earlier, the very meaning of being in the image of God is that we are accountable to God and can act only with his permission. How can we honour the creator if we destroy his creation?

The woven cord of relationship between humans, God and the rest of the natural world resurfaces again and again in scripture. The Old Testament is full of extravagant images of nature praising God, where mountains skip (Psalm 114:4) and trees clap their hands (Isaiah 55:12). Isaiah speaks of the coming of God's wise rule as a world in which 'the wolf shall live with the lamb, the leopard shall lie down with the kid… and a little child shall lead them' (Isaiah 11:6). This vision might just be picked up in an often-overlooked unique detail in Mark's account of Jesus in the wilderness, which notes that 'he was with the wild beasts' (Mark 1:13). There is nothing cosy about this – wild animals in those days included lions. The fascinating point is that Jesus was there and neither he nor the animals were harmed. Creation for a moment is back in harmony.

The lives of the Celtic saints are full of stories of harmony with nature. St Columba tells one of his monks to go to the beach to meet a visitor from Ireland. Expecting to find a boat, he finds instead an exhausted bird, which he tends back to health. St Cuthbert on one occasion kept a prayer vigil at night standing in the sea. When he returned to the shore, a pair of otters wrapped themselves around his painfully cold feet. My favourite story concerns St Kevin of Ireland, who would often pray with his arms stretched out in the shape of the cross. On one occasion, it is said that a bird landed on his upturned palm and he was so still that she laid an egg there. According to the story, Kevin stood where he was until the egg hatched. Of course, we have to distinguish history from legend, but there is an underlying message to these stories. These people whom we remember as saints because of their closeness to God and love for their fellow humans also had a gentleness which brought them into a harmony with wild creatures. The Kevin story reminds me that our relationship with the natural world is also one in which sometimes we have to inconvenience ourselves for the sake of other members of creation.

This is hardly something to which the present generation of humans gives much attention. Increasingly I find watching nature programmes an experience that leaves me sad. We have technology which allows us to get close to some of the most wonderful creatures on the planet, and yet every programme ends with a warning that in a few years' time these creatures may be lost for ever. Denial of the reality of climate change continues and, alarmingly, it is embraced by some of the most powerful people in the world in order to protect their wealth and power, but among the global scientific community it is beyond reasonable doubt. Earth Overshoot Day, calculated by the independent scientific think tank the Global Footprint Network, is the date on which humanity's resource consumption for the year exceeds the earth's capacity to regenerate those resources in that same year. In 1987, it was 19 December, meaning that we were still almost living within the earth's means. In 2021, it was 29 July and, other than a fallback in 2020 due to the pandemic, it has been getting earlier every year.

The most terrifying consequence of our present overconsumption is the release of carbon dioxide into the atmosphere, which is causing the temperature of our planet to rise. As this happens, the polar ice caps are beginning to melt. The ice caps help to keep the planet cool by reflecting the sun's rays back, so as they get smaller the sun's heat will have greater effect. In 100 years' time, the ice caps could be gone. If that happens, sea levels will rise dramatically. I live on a hill in London about 45 metres above sea level. According to one scientific projection, in 100 years' time, the site of my home could be underwater. Long before that happens, the entire country of Bangladesh will also be underwater. If we are worried about the current global refugee crisis, we might think about what we will do when 160 million people are looking for a new home. Even sooner than that, within the next 15 years, the destruction of natural habitats through human activity will mean that some of the most beautiful and iconic animals on our planet will have become extinct. We are on our way to creating a planet on which no one will ever see a wild rhinoceros, gorilla or tiger ever again.

If discipleship is about imitating Jesus, who walked without harm among the wild beasts, then celebration of and care for creation are an essential part of discipleship for everyone, not just the few Christian groups who are leading the way on creation care.[34] So what can we do?

It has been wisely said that, if you are going to change your life, you have to change something that you do every day. There are many things we can do on a daily basis to move from being part of the earth's problem to being part of God's solution. There is lots of practical advice to be found on the websites of A Rocha[35] and Green Christian, and in the writings of Christian environmentalist Ruth Valerio.[36]

Because our whole lifestyle is so bound up with consuming, it can seem overwhelming to try to think and act in a different way, so here are three ways to begin thinking about and planning some actions with the help of the resources above.

1   Use less energy. This is as simple as turning off lights when there is no one in the room, and turning off heating when there is no one in the house. Low-energy light bulbs are now easily available, and with gas and electricity prices rising so regularly, it will also save you money. Look for those offering renewable energy – in some cases it may well also be cheaper. Kerbside recycling is now widely available in the UK and in other countries, so make sure you use it. Think about your car the next time you change it. For a creation-conscious Christian, size, performance and image will not be the only factors. Look at buying an electric car, if financially feasible.

Look at fuel consumption. In London, the roads are crammed with SUVs ('Sports Utility Vehicles' or 4x4s). Most of these have high ground clearance for off-road performance and yet many are used for nothing more adventurous than the school run. What Car lists 4x4s from Audi, Land Rover, Mercedes, Porsche and Volvo in its list of the ten least fuel-efficient cars.[37] As well as not buying vehicles that literally do cost the earth, we can try to use public transport whenever possible or affordable, cycle, or walk. Get into the habit of offering lifts so that others don't have to use their cars – another way of practising hospitality. If your work or activities do involve a lot of travelling, as mine sometimes do, then make a carbon offset payment, which will be used to plant trees that will absorb some of the carbon dioxide released by our vehicles.[38] When it comes to white goods like fridges and cookers, always check the energy rating and go for the most economical you can afford.

2   Buy less stuff. This one is a bit obvious really and it also has the advantage of saving us money! When it comes to food, try to follow the LOAF principle: Local–Organic–Animal Friendly–Fairly Traded. It amazes me how many churches still don't serve fairly traded coffee but instead use brands which exploit their suppliers. When it comes to our own stuff, again other parts of this Way of Life link up. So many products today are deliberately not built to last: 'planned obsolescence' is the term. This is where the utility and beauty principle comes in again. If we can afford it, then it makes sense to buy items of high quality because we will have to replace them less often. This particularly applies to clothes, and remember that if you change your wardrobe regularly, charity shops and clothing banks will be delighted to have what you no longer need. Thankfully, as a result of environmental campaigning, supermarkets no longer dish out millions of free plastic bags which end up as litter, but do politely resist excess packaging wherever possible.

3   Don't support people who don't support the earth. Ultimately, whatever we do personally to live with integrity in an earth-friendly way will not be enough to hold back environmental catastrophe unless wider public opinion and political policies change. For that reason, it is a matter of conscience to get involved, whether by supporting campaigning organisations financially, going on marches, or getting involved in local politics. The impact of this came home to me several years ago at a local church election forum, to which I submitted a question about climate change. A candidate from one of the major parties began their answer by casting doubt on the science behind this. Immediately there was an audible intake of breath in the audience and a clear message that they were out of touch with something important. As Christians, we would not deliberately vote for politicians whose policies violated other people, and in the same way I suggest that we should not vote for those who in their priorities are callous towards God's creation. We should also check that our savings and investments are not being used unethically. Money talks, and we can take it away from those who use it badly.

All these kinds of actions are urgently required of all of us if we are going to stop the critical damage we are doing to our world, but they will all require effort because we will be swimming against the tide of global consumerism. Motivation is all-important and, in the end, we care most about what we love. That is why this waymark is called *celebrate* and care for creation. For many of us, the celebration of creation is already something that comes naturally. We love our visits to the countryside, our parks and our gardens, and every weekend tens of thousands of people head into the hills and mountains. Yesterday I was with a member of our church for whom I act as a Soul Friend. Before we talked, she showed me her garden, which she called her quiet place. It's a small high-walled area between the kitchen and the garage, set in a row of connected houses. It's deliberately low-maintenance with paving stones and a seat. In the middle are arrangements of natural stones and a number of miniature trees in pots grouped in threes.

Two large roads are just 100 metres away, yet this is an oasis and a place of prayer, where living nature points to its triune creator.

Others of us, separated from the soil, the birds and the animals by the habits of urban or suburban living, may need a little more help to reconnect, but, if we're disciples and imitators of Jesus 'in whom all things in heaven and earth were created… and in whom all things hold together' (Colossians 1:16–17), we will want to do that because somehow, in becoming more aware of them, we are getting closer to him. It starts with really simple things. You're almost at the end of this chapter. When you get there, put the book down and go outside (or stand in an open doorway if it's tipping down with rain). Just stop and deliberately take at least three breaths of fresh air. Look up at the sky and watch the movements of clouds if it's daytime, or the variety of how the stars appear if it's night. If you can see an animal or a bird, stop and watch it for a moment or so. Without realising it, you will have been doing exactly what God does all the time, the one who is aware of the life of every single sparrow (Luke 12:6). You'll come back inside feeling different. So, go and do it again tomorrow, and whenever you step out of the door, just breathe. Consciously or unconsciously you are celebrating with the creation which reflects God's glory and, even without words, praises him. Loving the creation helps us love our creator, and if we love our creator we will love his creation, and then, as never before, we will care for it.

To think about:

- In what ways do you intentionally pay attention to God's creation in order to appreciate it?

- What one change could you make now to live more sustainably?

For a group:

- Plan an evening celebrating God's creation, including silent listening for what God may be saying about our care of the world.

8

Waymark six:
heal whatever is broken

Jesus said, 'The Spirit of the Lord has anointed me to bring good news to the poor, to proclaim release to the captives and recovery of sight to the blind, to let the oppressed go free, to proclaim the year of the Lord's favour' (Luke 4:18–19). Paul wrote that 'through him God was pleased to reconcile to himself all things, whether on earth or in heaven, by making peace through the blood of his cross' (Colossians 1:20). St Irenaeus (second century) said, 'The glory of God is a human being fully alive.' In the name of Christ and through his power we pursue wholeness in body, mind and spirit for ourselves and for others. We seek to be peace makers between estranged individuals and in divided communities. We also pray for the 'healing of the land' in places polluted by human sinfulness (2 Chronicles 7:14).

Healing is a controversial subject. I have personally seen people healed from cancer and heroin addiction as a result of prayer. Yet our daughter, Emma, was born with profound and multiple handicaps. She died when she was five years old and we will carry the pain of that for the rest of our lives. We all live between the now and the not yet. We are those 'on whom the ends of the ages have come' (1 Corinthians 10:11). We live in the world as it is, what Paul calls 'the present evil age' (Galatians 1:4), but through Jesus we have begun to enter into 'the powers of the age to come' (Hebrews 6:5), the future in which eventually 'the creation itself will be set free from its bondage to decay and will obtain the freedom of the glory of the children of God' (Romans 8:21). We're not there yet, but we are on our way, and for that reason healing of people, places, relationships and communities is an integral part of this Way of Life.

God is the great healer. One of the fascinating things about our bodies which God has created is that when they are working properly, they self-heal. Physical damage grows back. Antibodies fight disease. Therefore, when we speak about healing we are not talking about something which goes against the grain of creation, but rather is working with it. Perhaps we need to be a little more careful when we talk about 'natural' and 'supernatural' – God doesn't seem to make these kinds of distinctions. Nevertheless, God does involve himself in his creation in ways that go beyond the normal healing processes, ways which we tend to describe as 'miraculous'. Early on in the journey out of Egypt, God makes polluted water drinkable. He describes himself as *Yahweh-Rapha*, 'I am the Lord who heals you' (Exodus 15:26). In the ancient Middle East, the revealing of a name was also a revealing of character and an entering into relationship. God is therefore saying that it's part of his nature to heal and that we may ask him to do that.

In New Testament Greek, the original language of these writings, the word meaning 'to save' or 'to bring to salvation', *sōzō*, also equally means 'to restore to health or make well'. This should not be too much of a surprise. The story of the Bible is the story of the creator God who out of love made all things, and when they became damaged and corrupted immediately set about restoring them. As we saw in the previous chapter, the final scene of the Bible is the new Jerusalem coming down to earth from heaven, where 'death will be no more; mourning and crying and pain will be no more, for the first things have passed away' (Revelation 21:1–4) and with its tree of life whose leaves are 'for the healing of the nations' (Revelation 22:2). Jesus announced the beginning of God's renewing rule on earth, what the Bible calls 'the kingdom of God,'[39] using very this-worldly language of healing and liberation from the book of Isaiah (Luke 4:16–19, Isaiah 61:1–4). He backed this up by beginning a ministry which very prominently included healing people from all kinds of physical problems and others that were characterised as 'demonic', and exercising a rule over nature which caused the stilling of storms and the multiplication of food. Before people ever got to grapple with the question of what Jesus being 'the Son of God' might mean, they would have seen and encountered him as a prophet and as a healer. This is now widely accepted in modern historical studies of Jesus, even by people who are sceptical about Christian faith itself.[40]

This takes us a vital stage further. Until the explosive growth of the Pentecostal and charismatic movements throughout the 20th century, many Christians regarded healing as something which may well have happened in the Bible and in the lives of some exceptionally gifted or saintly individuals down the centuries, but not something that would be experienced or practised in the mainstream life of the church. There are many reasons for this, but one of them was that we had lost sight of what the gospels are. It has now been demonstrated that they belong to the form of writing known as ancient biography and this affects how we read them.[41] Too often, Christians read the gospels as sources of Jesus' *teaching*, so when it comes to healing we look at what Jesus *said* about it. Ancient biographies, however, frequently described their subject in order that they might be *imitated* (and remember what we previously said discipleship is all about). That means that what Jesus *did* is just as important as what he said. We can find a trail of teaching which suggests that healing ought to be a normal feature of Christian life and ministry today: Jesus commissioned the twelve (Luke 9:1), then 70 others (Luke 10:1–9), to go out and heal, then told the apostles to pass on to future disciples everything he had taught them (Matthew 28:18–20), by implication including this. But far more immediate than this paper trail is the fact that Jesus himself healed, and as disciples we are called to imitate him.

So, what does this mean in practice? This Way of Life speaks of three different types of healing: that of people (including ourselves); places and communities; and relationships. Let's look at each of them.

Healing of people

When I first encountered the Christian healing ministry, my biggest problem in getting involved was worrying about what to do if nothing happened. It wasn't so much that I would look stupid (although that was a factor), but concern that someone else who was already unwell would feel totally let down and maybe lose any trust in God they had. There have been lots of books based on the New Testament describing different ways in which we should offer healing to people and there isn't space here to discuss them. Jesus and the apostles clearly had occasions when they were so in tune with the will of God that they could simply declare healing and it happened. That's something for us all to aim for, but it can seem quite daunting when you're just getting started. I find the approach described in James 5:13–18 the most help-ful, because it describes healing in the context where most of us will encounter it, that of the local church, and the approach is by means of hands-on prayer. Focusing on prayer reminds us that healing is God's work. In the words of the late John Wimber, who was powerfully used by God both in healing and in teaching others how to practise it,[42] 'No one has a miracle in their pocket.' We offer to pray for people, holding out the hope that God can do extraordinary things, but knowing that in this world, between the now and the not yet, this might result in physical healing but it is not guaranteed. James says that 'the prayer of faith will save the sick' (James 5:15), but recall that the word *sōzō* doesn't just mean physical healing.

Dr Chris Bird was one of the most important people in the life of my church. A university science lecturer, he had already helped found an educational charity, the Basotho Educational Trust, in one of the poor-est parts of Africa, and set out a vision for our church which enabled me to begin moving things forward when I arrived there. Barely a year later, and having just passed 40, he was diagnosed with inoperable cancer. One day Chris phoned me up and told me he had been writing down some reflections on his illness. As soon as I read them I asked him if he could share them with the church in a talk. With the congregation hanging on his every word, Chris explained how, since his diagnosis, he had been prayed for again and again. 'As I stand here today,' he said, 'I have not been cured. I still have cancer. But I have been healed in so many ways.' And he explained what they were.

I like to think of myself as a practical person. I know that not everyone I pray for will be healed. I've had the huge joy of seeing people with life-threatening illnesses get better, and people with deep inner disturbances that we might describe as 'demons' be set free. I also prayed with Chris just before he died, and I know personally what it feels like to have one of your own children die. If I concentrate on the doubts and the things I can't explain, I won't pray for anyone and no one will get healed. But if I pray for everyone I can, then some of them will get healed, and their lives, and this world, will be a better place. It's also hugely important to remember that, when Paul was describing the gifts of the Holy Spirit, he said that they are nothing without love (1 Corinthians 13:1–3). Healing is ultimately an expression of love for people who are hurting, damaged or limited in the functions of their bodies or minds. If love is our motive when we offer to pray for them, then they will receive something however the prayer is answered. I have never met anyone who regretted being prayed for, if it was done in love, whether or not they were ever healed. Local churches often practise healing ministry, and there are many other ways of learning how to get involved. Jesus did it and therefore we can do it. It's part of this Way of Life, so if you haven't already done so, take the first step to get involved.

Healing of places and communities

When you walk in the glens of the Scottish Highlands, you often pass broken stone walls or low rectangular grass-covered mounds. They are the remains of the croft houses of the people who were forcibly deported in the 18th and 19th centuries as part of the disgraceful episode in British history known as the Highland Clearances. I've seen them so often I barely notice them now. Hallaig is different. The remains of this village can be found on the Hebridean island of Raasay, a short ferry ride over from Skye. In 1746, most of the island was burned in reprisals for the failed Jacobite rebellion, but in June 1854, the village was emptied in a single day by the owner of the island, George Rainy, the merchant son of a church minister, who wanted the land for sheep. The uprooted people ended up in Australia, and their home remains a deserted ruin to this day. Hallaig is the saddest place I have ever visited. It's not just me. I later read the heart-breaking poem about it written by the great Gaelic poet Sorley Maclean, and translated into English by the Irish poet Seamus Heaney, who described Hallaig as 'a place that haunted me'. The grief of a lost people somehow lingers there.

I've felt a similar sense of profound inner disturbance visiting World War I battlefields in Flanders. My grandfather fought there and I've seen the massive memorial at Tyne Cot Cemetery listing the names of 300 of his regimental comrades who never came back. In just one afternoon, in an area where reminders of the trauma of a century ago can be seen everywhere, I had the uncanny and deeply distressing sensation that I was actually walking on crushed bones and of feeling what the Bible describes as violently shed blood 'crying out from the ground' (Genesis 4:10). I was conscious even then, despite open borders, of how deeply divided Europe still was, how old wounds were still open and old hatreds still alive. How much more so now?

I suspect many of us may have felt things like this at different times, but not been sure what to make of them. We know that places are important in the Bible: Jesus and others deliberately went and prayed in deserts and on mountains, but there has not been much reflection on why they are important. American writer Belden Lane has explored the healing power of wilderness[43] and in the Community of Aidan and Hilda we know that there is something very special about Holy Island, where people seem simply to encounter God in unexpected ways. The Old Testament speaks of the importance of land, which can become cursed and unproductive as a result of human sinfulness (Genesis 3:17–19), and God also promises that when his people turn to him he will 'heal their land' (2 Chronicles 7:14) and make it fertile again. In the New Testament, talk of the land is broadened out to embrace the whole earth and so these promises of healing can also be expanded.[44]

Healing of places can be as simple as responding to the intuitions we have when we are there. If it is a good place, then we could pray a blessing upon it (see Deuteronomy 26:15 as an example). If we sense something hurt, broken or disturbing in a place then we could ask God to bring healing there, following the example in 2 Chronicles 7. Sometimes we also need to be the answer to our own prayers. Whether a place is literally polluted or littered, or whether it is home to a dys- functional, damaged and damaging community, there may well be all sorts of practical things we can do to make it cleaner and better. There is also a much deeper dimension in respect of how the past history of a place can affect what is going on now. As you might expect, there are a variety of understandings of how this happens and what we can do about it, but the work and writings of Russ Parker, a member of our Community and director of the Acorn Christian Healing Foundation from 1995 to 2013, offer a good place to start.[45] For many of us, the first personal application of this part of the Way of Life may be simply to begin learning more about the spirituality of places.

Healing of relationships

This is another area in which different parts of the Way of Life flow into one another. What has already been said about forgiveness and reconciliation in the chapter about living simply all applies here. Here is also the place to remember that Jesus said, 'Blessed are the peacemakers' (Matthew 5:9). An important way of showing love for others is being prepared to step in and defuse arguments and conflicts between them. Christians are as capable of getting angry as anyone else, sometimes more so because too many of us refuse to be honest about what we are really feeling and bottle up our emotions until they explode all over someone else. I have sometimes seen a room full of people sitting in appalled silence as two people shout at each other when if just a couple of them had called for calm it would have taken the heat out of the situation much more quickly.

A final word on forgiveness and reconciliation concerns situations in which any kind of abuse is taking place. As I explained previously, forgiveness is primarily about us and our feelings, whereas reconciliation is about a relationship with someone else. Neither of these things mean that we should tolerate or cover up abusive behaviour. Allowing an abuser to continue to abuse is not loving towards them because they never have to confront their behaviour, and may endanger us if we do not seek protection. Jesus could be very confrontational when someone else's well-being was threatened (e.g. John 7:53—8:11).

Healing of ourselves

Healing starts with us. For all that God calls us into his great mission to heal the world, his greatest desire for each of us is that we are remade in the image of Christ. It's true that we are now defined by the cross and resurrection and not by our past. It is true that in Christ each of us is a new creation (2 Corinthians 5:17), but just like the rest of creation we still live between the now and the not yet. As John puts it, 'We are God's children now; what we will be has not yet been revealed. What we do know is this; when he is revealed, we will be like him' (1 John 3:2–3). We are all shaped, consciously or unconsciously, by our experiences in life, and coming to faith in Christ does not automatically erase the past even though it does change our relationship to it. We will all have learned ways of thinking, feeling and acting which are not what Jesus would do. Many of us will also have had painful, even traumatic, experiences which have left us inwardly damaged. When people hurt others, it's so often because they themselves are hurting. One of the challenges of this Way of Life is to face up honestly to our own need for healing, but we can do so safely because we are in the care of the greatest possible physician of spirit, mind and body. Sometimes prayer and self-help are enough. Sometimes, and a warning indicator is when we see that our reaction to a situation has become more of a problem than the situation itself, we may need the help of a counsellor or psychotherapist.

Too often we have been conditioned into thinking it's weak to ask for help, or that we are not trusting God enough if we need someone else to help us. Here's something I found helpful. We often think of military special forces as being incredibly tough and self-sufficient, pressing on at all costs and tolerating no weakness. I'm told that in small patrols, if one member is in difficulty, they are trained to tell the others immediately so that the team can help each other before it becomes a dangerous crisis. God wants to heal us. He has given us other people who can help us if we need them. The result of our own healing is greater empathy for others and an increased capacity to share in God's work of healing.

To think about:

- Is prayer for healing (for others) part of your practice, and if not, what steps could you take to learn more?

- Prayerfully ask if there is anything in your inner world that needs healing (you may already know), and if so, what steps might you take to begin to get help?

For a group:

- Take a walk together around your area, alert to what you see and hear, and to your intuitions. Pray God's blessing on whatever seems positive and healing for whatever seems broken.

9

Waymark seven:
be open to the Holy Spirit and listen

Jesus told his disciples, 'When the Spirit of truth comes, he will guide you into all the truth' (John 16:13). He also spoke of the Spirit as the wind which blows wherever it chooses (John 3:8). Some Celtic Christian missionaries had such faith in the leading of the Spirit that they were willing to put to sea in small coracles, and go where the wind took them! Whether as a gentle breeze or a wild wind, we seek the same kind of openness to the leading of the Spirit. We cultivate a willingness to let God move us beyond where we are comfortable and into what is new or unfamiliar.

The New Testament gift of prophecy has an important part to play in this. This is the spiritual gift of receiving insights from God which build up, encourage, console, guide or challenge ourselves or others. Paul encourages all Christians to desire this gift (1 Corinthians 14:1). Such insights must be carefully weighed (1 Thessalonians 5:20–21), and learning to listen to God is a skill that requires time. We seek to cultivate an inner stillness which can distinguish the voice of God from all the other 'voices' and influences within us. We also listen for God's voice through scripture and through his creation.

The Bible begins with God creating. We are told right at the start that his Spirit was at work in this process,[46] and that in order to bring things into being God simply spoke. The new creation brought about by Jesus' death and resurrection explodes into life on the day of Pentecost when the Holy Spirit is poured out upon the disciples, through whom God speaks to the crowd in such a way that each one heard them speaking in their native language (Acts 2:1–11). God's Spirit and God's speaking belong together, and yet too often his people either do not want to hear, or have never learned how to listen. 'When I spoke to you persistently, you did not listen, and when I called you, you did not answer' (Jeremiah 7:13), says God again and again in the book of Jeremiah, as he tries to divert his people away from disaster. In similar circumstances, Jesus warns his audience to 'pay attention to how you listen; for to those who have, more will be given; and from those who do not have, even what they seem to have will be taken away' (Luke 8:18). The Bible is nothing if not a record of God speaking to people. The Acts of the Apostles, which takes up the story after Jesus' resurrection and ascension, has sometimes been called 'the Acts of the Holy Spirit' because the spread of the message of Jesus and the growth of the church are at every stage guided and energised by the activity of the Spirit. We probably need to be careful about saying that some of the more extraordinary events of the New Testament should be 'normal' in the church today, but it is equally clear that our experience of the Holy Spirit today should not in any way be less than what we see in people then.

If your experience of Christianity has been through a church which identifies itself as Pentecostal, charismatic or Full Gospel, then little of this needs explaining. Nevertheless, for many Christians today the Holy Spirit is still the overlooked person of the Trinity, often mentioned but frequently misunderstood. Your experience may well have been something like mine. I come from a non-church background and, while I was never an atheist, the idea that you could have some kind of personal relationship with God was entirely new to me. The first church that I joined was very good at teaching me the basics of being a Christian, especially the importance of personal prayer and Bible reading. The rhythms of my walk with God were set in motion there right at the very beginning. They were also very insistent that faith did not depend on feelings, but this was emphasised to such an extent that any idea that God might be experienced in a felt way was discouraged. It seemed that Jesus did miracles 2,000 years ago but we should not expect them to happen now, and if we expected God to speak in any way except through the Bible, then we would be seriously led astray. When I was 18 I met people who talked about the Holy Spirit in a totally different way. They claimed to have experienced God's love and power and gifts in a way which went far beyond anything I had been led to expect. They also seemed to be a lot more alive in their relationship with God than I had ever been. I knew there was something more but I didn't really know what it was. I kept asking for more from God and reading stuff about the Spirit, but didn't understand it because it was outside my experience. One day, God changed that. I experienced his presence, his power and the sheer joy of knowing him in a way I had never known before. My relationship with God changed immediately. It was like moving from black and white into colour.

How we experience the presence of God varies enormously from person to person and it is as much down to our personality as anything else. The great 18th-century preacher John Wesley famously spoke of the life-changing moment when his heart was 'strangely warmed' by God, assuring him that he was indeed truly a child of God, yet he said that he never experienced the depths of joy which many of his converts found. Nevertheless, Romans 5:5 says that 'God's love has been poured into our hearts through the Holy Spirit'. It is hard to think of any interpretation of these words that does not in some way imply that we feel or experience something, and it is absolutely clear that Paul means this to be the experience of every Christian. Likewise, he goes on to speak of the Spirit 'bearing witness with our spirit that we are children of God' (Romans 8:16). Again, this speaks of an encounter with God which leads to us knowing at the deepest level of our being that he is now a father to us. If you're reading this and thinking that you have never really sensed what it is to be loved by God, or to feel assured that you really are in relationship with God, then the first step in following this waymark is to begin asking God to reveal himself to you more deeply. Leave the answer and the timing up to him. You may have to repeatedly ask, seek and knock (Luke 11:9–13), as I had to, but God will definitely answer.

As we grow in openness to the Spirit, so we will find that God has been trying to speak to us all along, but now our ability to hear him will grow sharper. The first waymark highlights how God speaks to us through scripture (and nothing we think God is saying to us will ever be at variance with what is taught in the Bible) and also through creation. There is also another very important way in which God speaks.

Paul describes many different gifts of the Holy Spirit, and gives four sample lists (Romans 12:6–8; 1 Corinthians 12:4–11; 1 Corinthians 12:27–31; Ephesians 4:11–13). Only one gift features in all four lists, and it is a gift called prophecy. Most of us tend to think of prophecy as prediction, being able to foresee accurately something which will happen in the future. A lot of biblical prophecy is like that, especially the great Old Testament books of Isaiah, Jeremiah and Ezekiel (and many of the so-called 'minor prophets'), which are repeatedly warning the Israelites that if they do not stop being unfaithful to God and progressing into deeper and deeper corruption and oppression of others, the result will be conquest by the powerful Assyrian and Babylonian empires and exile from their God-given land. This, by the way, is what happened, but then God spoke to them again during the exile in prophecies recorded later in Isaiah (chapters 40—55) telling them that he would bring them home again. That also happened.

Much biblical prophecy, however, is as much about forth-telling as it is about foretelling. One of my favourite examples concerns the period after the Israelites returned from exile in the sixth century BC. Jerusalem and its temple were in ruins and they had to rebuild, but the work got bogged down and the people became distracted and discouraged. God sent them a prophet called Haggai who encouraged them to get started again. When they did, God gave them one of the shortest prophetic messages in the Bible: 'I am with you, says the Lord' (Haggai 1:13). That was all they needed to hear. While God does still speak about the future, the New Testament gift of prophecy often seems to be about receiving God's word for us or for others right now. Paul writes that 'those who prophesy speak to other people for their building up and encouragement and consolation' (1 Corinthians 14:3) and, while he says that an attitude of love is essential, he urges us to seek after the gifts of God's Spirit, 'and especially that you may prophesy' (1 Corinthians 14:1).

So how does this work in practice? Often in the Bible God seems to speak in very dramatic and unmistakable ways such as visions and dreams, an audible voice, or visits from angels. There is no reason to think such things would never happen now. The lives of the Celtic saints are full of such stories and I have met a number of people who have converted to Christianity from Islam, for example, as a result of God speaking to them in one of these very direct ways. Nevertheless, these things are unusual and there seem to be more common ways in which God speaks. Acts 13 describes an important meeting of the church in Antioch, at which, significantly, several people described as 'prophets' were present. They seem to have gathered to spend some time seeking God's will, and 'while they were worshipping the Lord and fasting, the Holy Spirit said, "Set apart for me Barnabas and Saul for the work to which I have called them"' (Acts 13:2). The result was the beginning of the missionary work of Paul, previously known as Saul. But how did the Holy Spirit speak?

The experience of many Christians is that God often speaks to us through our normal thought processes. We think in a variety of different ways, sometimes in words, sometimes in images, and sometimes we work on more intuitive levels – we just 'know' something. Sometimes, and not surprisingly, it often happens when we are praying; we will find that some words, or an image, or an intuition, stand out in our thoughts in a way that seems to be addressing us or other people, or a particular situation. It's significant that the word 'inspiration', which we use to describe the moment when we get an idea, literally carries the sense of being breathed into, and, as we have already seen, in the Bible the word for 'breath' and the word for 'Spirit' are the same.

So far, so good; but how do we then tell the difference between something that is just an idea in our mind and something which is actually a message from God? How do we avoid making mistakes which might have serious consequences for ourselves or other people? The first thing is to understand that no one today has the authority of an Old Testament prophet, which enables them to go around saying 'thus says the Lord' and being right all the time. 'We know only in part, and we prophesy only in part,' says Paul in 1 Corinthians 13:9. That means we can get it wrong when we think God is speaking to us.

The second thing we therefore need to do is to 'weigh what is said' (1 Corinthians 14:29), striking the balance between not ignoring prophecy but at the same time testing everything (compare 1 Thessalonians 5:20–21). God will not contradict himself, so if it seems that he is telling us something which does not sound like the kind of thing Jesus would say or do, then we have probably got it wrong. This is an important principle, because some of us have a very talkative inner critic who is constantly putting us down. Paul urges us to 'speak the truth in love' (Ephesians 4:15) and to restore those who have done wrong 'in a spirit of gentleness' (Galatians 6:1). We can therefore expect God to act in the same way.

The third way of recognising whether something is a message from God is to make the distinction between revelation, interpretation and application. Put simply, revelation means the words or the picture or the intuition which we think might have come from God. What exactly did we 'see' or 'hear' or 'sense'? Sometimes something will come vividly into our minds but we do not immediately know what it means. This is why prophecy is a gift best used with other people where we can share what we think God might be saying. It might mean something to someone else, or others may be able to help work out what it means – this is the interpretation stage. I heard of a person in a prayer meeting who kept seeing in her mind a vivid image of a large lorry with the word 'macaroni' on the side. With great embarrassment she shared this thought, only to discover another woman had a son about whom she was very worried, who was a lorry driver, and you can guess what he regularly transported. The third stage, application, means thinking through the implications and consequences of something God might be saying and deciding how best to act.

If all this sounds complicated, don't be put off. In my entire life as a Christian, God has never led me to make a fool of myself (I don't need any help with that). Jesus said that, as he was the good shepherd, his sheep would 'know his voice' (John 10:3–5). With practice, we learn how to recognise the voice of Jesus among all the other voices we may be hearing, and this leads into another important element of this waymark, the practice of silence.

We are so used to the number of times the Bible calls on us to praise God that we often overlook the significance of meeting God in silence. Amid the chaos of war comes the counter-intuitive command to 'be still, and know that I am God' (Psalm 46:10). Another prayer in distress begins, 'For God alone my soul waits in silence; from him comes my salvation' (Psalm 62:1). When Elijah escapes to Horeb, the mountain of God, physically and emotionally exhausted, God mirrors his inner turmoil with a storm and an earthquake, but only meets him in 'sheer silence' (1 Kings 19:12). Although God definitely reveals himself in Jesus, the living Word, there is also a strand of scripture which says that when we draw near to God, at some point we reach a place where words are inadequate and only silence remains. 'The Lord is in his holy temple; let all the earth keep silence before him,' proclaims the prophet Habakkuk (Habakkuk 2:20). In Revelation, we are presented with Jesus, the Lamb of God, enthroned in glory opening the final seal as God's plan to heal and restore creation comes to its completion. 'When the Lamb opened the seventh seal, there was silence in heaven' (Revelation 8:1). There is literally nothing more to say.

'Silence is the gateway to the soul and the soul is the gateway to God,' says Christopher Jamison, former Abbot of Worth Abbey, and presenter of the TV series *The Monastery* and *The Big Silence* in which ordinary people had a taste of Christian contemplative prayer. The Celtic and desert Christians fully understood this. People like Columba, Aidan,

Hilda and Cuthbert lived busy, demanding lives as missionaries and leaders of communities, yet they regularly took time out – a lot of time – to be with God in silence. This might just have something to do with why they were such effective people.

It's easy to confuse silence with peace and tranquillity. It's often anything but that. In today's world, we are so used to noise, or at least background music, that total silence can quickly become disorientating and unsettling. The first thing most people experience when they first try silent prayer is the amount of noise going on in their head. Thoughts race to the front of our minds and as fast as we push them away, they race back again, bringing their friends with them. I found this crushingly frustrating. I read books on silent prayer which said things like, 'Just let your thoughts and anxieties slip away.' The reality was that they just jumped up and shouted in my face. Then I read about St Anthony of Egypt, often seen as one of the founders of the desert movement in fourth-century Egypt. Anthony felt called to radical simplicity so he gave up his possessions to go and be alone in a cave and pray. He walked straight into a psychological war zone. The account of his life says he was regularly assaulted by demons and fought intense battles against them. Part of this prolonged temptation seems to be Anthony being brought face-to-face with himself and what lay deep within him. He emerged a changed man to whom others flocked for spiritual guidance.

Silence, whether through Christian contemplative prayer or the techniques of mindfulness meditation, first reveals what is really going on inside us. I used to think 'distractions' in prayer were to be overcome and pushed away. I now realise that I need to pay attention to them because they might be telling me something. Many of us never pay attention to this inner world, and as a result anything God is saying to us can so easily get caught up with our own desires, fears and ambitions. Silence helps us, first of all, to know ourselves, but then, as we practise it regularly, we start to grow in awareness that our thoughts and feelings are, as many writers have expressed it, simply like the changing weather on a mountain: wind, rain, sunshine and snow, which pass by hour by hour. Behind them is the unchanging mountain itself, God, who is the one in whom we live and move and have our being.

When it comes to contemplative prayer, I feel as if I am only in the foothills, barely even on the mountain. What I have learned with gratitude is that the charismatic movement gave us back the gift of prophecy, but the monastic movements teach us discernment as we learn to untangle the voice of God from our own ego. David Cole's book, *The Mystic Path of Meditation*, mentioned in chapter four, is a great place to start in learning to pray in this way, and Martin Laird's *Into The Silent Land: The practice of contemplation* is also full of useful insights and practical advice.[47] Being open to the Spirit requires us to resist relentless busyness in the trust that waiting on God really will bring us to a better way. As someone once said: 'Don't just do something; sit there.'

To think about:

- When do you think God has been speaking to you? If you can, recall and reflect on what God seemed to be saying.

- Experiment with silence. Set a timer for four minutes and silently repeat the words, 'Lord Jesus Christ, have mercy'[48], no matter what else is going on in your head. Keep trying regularly and see what happens.

For a group:

- Experiment with prophecy. Pray for each person, asking yourself what a loving God might want to say to them. Share what comes (even if you don't understand it) and celebrate the encouragements people receive.

10

Waymark eight:
pray for good to overcome evil

Jesus proclaimed the arrival of the kingdom of God. He taught his disciples to pray for its coming on earth as it is in heaven. We commit ourselves to praying for the coming of God's just and merciful rule in the situations and concerns that we encounter, following the example of Cuthbert and others who 'stormed the gates of heaven' with persevering prayer. We understand that as we do so we will sometimes encounter opposition and we recognise the existence of spiritual forces of evil (John 12:31, Ephesians 6:10–18). Prayer is central in overcoming them. We do not project onto this unseen dimension things for which human beings need to take responsibility, but we do seek to discern the spiritual influences at work. Such prayer is always related to positive action because our ultimate goal is to 'overcome evil with good' (Romans 12:21).[49]

'War – what's it good for? Absolutely nothing!' Most Christians would agree with that old Motown song. One publisher has produced a hymn book in which even well-known classics have had any military language edited out. We call Jesus the prince of peace. We know that he denounced violence. We know that he submitted to torture and death. Yet Jesus' teaching is full of the language of conflict, and it's right at the heart of his teaching on prayer.

We have already seen that Jesus and his disciples, following the practices of Jews in the Old Testament, had a well-established daily rhythm
of prayer, and that this rhythm was also practised by Peter, Paul and
the early Christians. Yet the disciples still asked Jesus, 'Lord, teach
us to pray, as John taught his disciples' (Luke 11:1). None of John
the Baptist's teaching on prayer has survived, but we have one clue.
Because John came from the wilderness, some scholars think he might
have had contact with the separatist Jews of the Qumran community,
who had their own ideas about the kind of future God would bring.
The Dead Sea Scrolls, which they wrote, contain many of their own
distinctive prayers, so it's entirely possible that John taught ways of
praying which reflected his own message. Jesus did the same. His core
message, proclaimed, illustrated and enacted, was that 'the kingdom
of God has come near' (Mark 1:15) or, as Tom Wright put it in more
modern language, God has become king on earth as in heaven,[50] and
this message is at the heart of his distinctive teaching on prayer.

The prayer we call the Lord's Prayer (Luke 11:1–4 and Matthew 6:9–13)
begins with worship and moves on to asking God to meet our needs
and forgive our sins (with a more challenging bit about also forgiving
others). This is the typical stuff many of us pray about every day, but
in between the praise and the petitions comes a prayer for God's reign
to be established and God's will to be done on earth as in heaven, and
after the other requests comes a prayer for protection against a time
of evil attack. In his distinctive teaching on prayer, Jesus doesn't just
want us to know that God is our loving Father, he also wants us to share
God's love for his world by praying that his will may begin to be done
in all the places where that is not yet happening.

We're frequently, and rightly, told that there is more to prayer than
just asking God for things, but at the same time I have found that
some Christians feel quite awkward about asking God for anything.
They feel either that it's selfish, especially if it's something relating to
them, or else that there is a danger that they are trying to make God fit
their personal agenda. This is where it is so important to be aware of
what Jesus said about prayer. In the first place, he tells us that God is

a father who gives good gifts to his children (Luke 11:13). If our motives are wrong or we're asking for something we don't need, then we can trust God to deal with that the right way. The overwhelming encouragement of scripture is that 'in everything by prayer and supplication with thanksgiving let your requests be made known to God' (Philippians 4:6). Go ahead and ask! Second, in his parable of the vine and the branches, Jesus says that 'those who abide in me and I in them bear much fruit, because apart from me, you can do nothing' (John 15:5). That verse means exactly what it says, and the most obvious way of showing that we are indeed relying on Jesus is to pray about everything we seek to do in his name. In our church council meetings, we have prayer as the first and last item on the agenda so that it is formally part of the meeting along with the other 'business'. We allocate at least ten minutes to that first prayer item and deliberately name before God every item on the agenda. We often read John 15:1–5 as part of that.

Praying for others and praying for our Christian ministries and missions is only the beginning of our praying. Paul urged that 'supplications, prayers, intercessions and thanksgivings should be made for everyone, for kings and all who are in high positions, so that we may lead a quiet and peaceable life in all godliness and dignity' (1 Timothy 2:1–2). When we wonder how we should pray for leaders with whom we may strongly disagree, it's worth bearing in mind that Paul lived during the reign of the depraved and possibly insane Emperor Caligula and was eventually executed by Nero. He prayed for them and urged others to do the same.

We can go even further in our praying. In Romans 8, Paul speaks about the suffering of creation, which groans in labour pains as it waits for God to set it free from decay (vv. 19–22). As part of that creation, we also groan as in different ways we share in the suffering of the world. Then comes one of the most encouraging statements about prayer in the whole Bible: 'We do not know how to pray as we ought,' Paul says (v. 26). Many of us will feel that is a massive understatement! Then comes the good news: 'The Spirit helps us in our weakness... And God... knows what is the mind of the Spirit... [who] intercedes for the saints' (vv. 26–27). At the simplest level this says that the very act of trying to pray, even if we cannot put into words what we want to say, is still effective because as we pray the Spirit prays in and through us. Then there's the deeper level. Creation groans, we groan and 'the Spirit intercedes with sighs too deep for words' (v. 26). We pray not just for ourselves, not just for the wider human community, but for creation itself.

In the Anglican church to which I belong, our main acts of worship include a section called 'Prayers of Intercession', which often begins with the words 'Let us pray for the church and for the world, and let us thank God for his goodness'. Week by week, month by month, year by year, we bring before God what is going on in the wider world. The needs never seem to stop coming and sometimes it's tempting to wonder what difference our prayers actually make. I remind myself that the world could be a whole lot worse, and it might just be so if we stopped praying. When I became a Christian, half of Europe was still dominated by communism. In our church youth group, we prayed regularly for the 'Siberian Seven', a family of Russian Christians who took refuge from persecution in the American Embassy and were trapped there for five years. Eventually they were allowed to leave, but just a few years later, to the amazement of the world, the Berlin Wall came down and the seemingly all-powerful communist regimes disintegrated.

A few years ago, at a Community of Aidan and Hilda national event, we hosted some Christians from Burma, at the time one of the most oppressive military regimes in the world. The man was an exile because of his political activities. The woman was a campaigner within the country for women's rights. In Burma, women's rights meant not being raped by the army. We asked what we could do to support them. They told us there were three things. We could provide aid, as one member of our Community already did in supporting Christian refugees who had fled over the Thai border. We could also protest, using our democratic rights to urge our government to put pressure on the Burmese leaders. Then they told us there was a third thing we could do, which would be far more effective than either of the other two, and the only thing that would ultimately make a difference. That was to pray. When I am tempted to doubt whether praying is worth it, I remember these two people who were literally risking their lives in the cause of justice and Jesus, and if they tell me the most effective thing I can do is pray, then I will go on praying.

This kind of prayer is not about telling God what to do. It's about looking around and in every situation where what we see does not look like the kind of thing God would want, we ask for God's just and merciful rule to be expressed there. In the inspiring lives of the Celtic Christians, there are many stories about prayer. The great missionary Bishop Cuthbert is often given as an example both for the duration of his praying (he often spent whole nights in prayer), and also for the intensity with which he prayed. The historian Bede tells us that, when Cuthbert presided over the breaking of bread and sharing of wine, he would often shed tears as he remembered the sacrifice of Jesus. On another occasion, he and his companions ran out of food when their boat was driven onto a remote shore in a winter storm. Remembering that God fed the Israelites in another kind of wilderness, Cuthbert urged his group to 'storm heaven with prayers'. A day later they found food. I sometimes wonder if some of our praying is too polite. We don't need to shout in order for God to hear us, but equally if we care deeply about something it will show in the way we speak about it.

My favourite example is Cuthbert's predecessor, Aidan, the quietly spoken Irishman who came to England from Scotland to bring the good news of Jesus to its people, and whose mission base on Lindisfarne became the cradle-place of English Christianity. Incredibly, for such a significant person who spent a huge amount of time in prayer, we have only one description of him praying. Aidan would go to pray alone on Farne Island out in the North Sea. On one occasion while he was there, an army from the hostile neighbouring kingdom of Mercia, led by their king, Penda, laid siege to the Northumbrian capital of Bamburgh. They tore down outlying houses and used the wood to try to burn down the town walls. Two miles out to sea, Aidan saw the smoke. Bede tells us that 'he raised his eyes and hands towards heaven and said with tears, "O Lord, see how much evil Penda is doing."[51] In answer to this breathtakingly simple prayer, the wind turned and blew the flames back towards the Mercians, who withdrew in confusion. We actually do not have to do anything more complicated than telling God what the need is and asking him to do something about it. Any of us can do that and part of this Way of Life is that we commit to doing so regularly. If it helps us to make lists, there is nothing unspiritual about doing that. God has asked us to bring to him the needs of his world.

As we pray about particular situations, our practice of being open to the Spirit may mean that we gain insight into how to pray in more specific ways. In the Old Testament, two of the godliest representatives of the Israelites, Ezra the priest and Daniel the prophet, both prayed for their people, identifying themselves with their sins as if they had also committed them (Ezra 9:1—10:1; Daniel 9:1–19). Community of Aidan and Hilda members in Australia and the USA have taken part in representative acts of repentance for the theft of land by their ancestors from aboriginal and first-nation peoples.

As we pray on, we may find ourselves not only identifying with the hurt and pain of others in order through the Spirit to express it to God, but also coming into an awareness of the forces of evil at work in the world.

A very important strand in Jesus' understanding of how God's rule would come on earth as in heaven, one which many modern Christians find strange and uncomfortable, was that there was a power opposed to God. Most other Jews saw the pagan Romans as this power, but Jesus insisted that trying to fight them was missing the point because the real enemy lay hidden behind them. Jesus frequently referred to this enemy as Satan and saw his sacrificial death and resurrection as the way this evil would be overcome. 'This is your hour, and the power of darkness,' he told those who came to arrest him (Luke 22:53). Earlier in the week he had spoken of his death more indirectly but with the bold claim that through it 'the ruler of this world will be driven out' (John 12:31). Paul shared this world view. Writing to the Ephesians in the city that was one of the centres of pagan religion with its huge temple of Diana-Artemis, and in the eastern part of the Roman Empire where the worship of the emperor as a god was first taking hold, he tells them that 'our struggle is not against flesh and blood, but against the rulers, against the authorities, against the powers of this dark world and against the spiritual forces of evil in the heavenly realms' (Ephesians 6:12).

For most of the modern era, remembering the witch hunts of previous centuries when people were tortured and murdered in the belief that they were allied with Satan, this kind of material in the Bible was side-lined or ignored as being an unfortunate hangover from a more primitive age. After World War II, theologians suddenly became interested in evil again. No one could understand how a nation which had been at the forefront of European civilisation and the spread of Christianity internationally could have so quickly turned into depraved dealers of death and destruction who had tried to exterminate an entire race. The idea that human actions could somehow be influenced by powers of evil regained credibility.

Christians today differ in how we understand these things. Some believe in Satan and other demonic powers as actual non-physical beings, less powerful than God but still able to have a destructive influence in the material world. Others, like the American theologian Walter Wink, think in terms of the spirituality of organisations, communities or countries, which can become toxic and in effect take on a life of its own.

While Jesus and the apostles dealt directly with what they discerned as demonic interference in individuals, there does not seem to be any indication in the New Testament of a similar approach to the powers on a larger level. In fact, the focus of the whole Bible is on God and not on Satan. Earlier in Ephesians, Paul explains that 'through the church the wisdom of God' is 'made known to the rulers and authorities' (Ephesians 3:10) and the main way he sees this happening is through Christians living and sharing the good news of Jesus. Significantly, the later discussion of the powers of darkness with its famous image of the armour of God ends with a call to 'pray in the Spirit at all times in every prayer and supplication' (Ephesians 6:18).

There is sometimes a fear that any kind of belief in the demonic will lead us back into demonising people and treating them as inherently evil and as enemies to be destroyed. Actually, I think it has the opposite effect. From a human perspective, when I look at the hate-driven fanaticism of IS and similar groups, it seems that only overwhelming military force can stop them – violence overcoming violence. If I consider that their anger at injustices, inflamed by ideologies which provide convenient enemies to blame, is like an open wound which has become infected by a greater evil that simply glories in destruction, then I can see another way. Colossians 2:15 tells me that through the cross Jesus disarmed this power of evil, and that, if I pray in his name, those in its grip can still be set free.

We are called to live as people of God's kingdom and to pray for the coming of God's kingdom. Both are essential and this Way of Life is about enabling us to do both more effectively, but I think one of our biggest challenges is to grasp afresh just how important it is to pray regularly for the church, the world and all creation, as much as we do for ourselves, our families and our friends.

To think about:

- What part does praying for the wider world have in your personal rhythm of prayer?

- What is your understanding of the powers of darkness and how does that influence the way you think and pray?

For a group:

- Discuss different ways in which you might pray about a major local, national or international situaion, then pray together about it.

11

Waymark nine:
pursue unity

Jesus said, 'I will draw all people to myself' (John 12:32), and prayed that his disciples, both then and now, 'may all be one' (John 17:20–21). Paul taught that we should all regard ourselves as members of the one body of Christ (1 Corinthians 12:12). The church today is marred by divisions between eastern and western traditions, Protestants and Roman Catholics, and many other smaller splits. In the Celtic period, the distinctive features of these different strands of Christianity were still woven together. The early church in Britain had the emphasis on scripture and mission reflected today by Evangelicals, the emphasis on incarnation and sacraments reflected by Catholics and the emphasis on the Spirit and the Trinity reflected by Pentecostals and Orthodox. It held in balance both the contemplative and the active life. The Celtic missionaries also adapted themselves to the culture, patterns and practices of the society they sought to reach for Christ. Aidan rejected anything that would make him superior to or separate from the people. Hilda was regarded as a spiritual mother by many ordinary people.

Our first expression of unity is by making it a priority to worship and meet regularly with the other members of our own church fellowship. We also seek to welcome all Christians as fellow travellers with Christ, to express solidarity with them by actions as well as words, and to emphasise the things that unite us while we seek to overcome those which still divide us. We seek to cultivate solidarity with all people in everything, except sin, and to value and affirm what is good in all people and cultures. We seek to identify and remove attitudes and practices which create barriers between church and people. We act to overcome divisions based on gender, colour or social status, wherever we find them.

One of the things I love about Jesus is his attitude towards other people. That really offended Jesus' enemies because they didn't approve of the people he chose to sit and eat with. Food was one of the things that defined a Jew and, in their culture, to eat with someone implied acceptance of them and relationship with them. Jesus sat down with tax collectors whose only priority was to fill their quota of the hated Roman poll tax by whatever means, with sex workers, and with people just labelled as 'sinners': those who had given up or dropped out from following the Jewish law with any devotion. He also challenged gender stereotypes in his attitude to women, and crossed racial barriers by associating with Samaritans, who were hated as mixed-race semi-pagans, and with Gentiles from the oppressing majority culture. He even ate with Pharisees, when invited, even though they were his most bitter opponents. These people actively wanted to be with Jesus, so we can assume that he made them feel comfortable with him rather than condemned.

How well do we Christians today measure up? Years ago, I read a parody of the old hymn 'Onward, Christian Soldiers':

Like a mighty tortoise, moves the church of God;
Brothers we are treading where we've always trod.
We are all divided, many bodies we,
Very strong on doctrine, weak on charity.

I'd like to think we'd made some progress, but I'm not so sure. The world in which we live at the moment is deeply divided over race, religion, nationality, politics, class, gender and sexuality, and these divisions seem to be deepening and becoming more and more hateful. The calling of the church is to be the place where 'there is no longer Jew or Greek, there is no longer slave or free, there is no longer male and female; for all of you are one in Christ Jesus' (Galatians 3:28). Writing at the end of the second century, the apologist Tertullian argued for the truth of Christianity by pointing to the radical way in which Christians treated one another. 'See how these Christians love one another,' people would say. More than ever, a divided world needs a united church if the healing, reconciling message of Jesus is going to be taken seriously and allowed to have its effect.

Christianity is irreducibly something we do together. We are described as members of the household of God, brothers and sisters of Jesus and each other, and parts of the body of Christ. In the New Testament, the word 'you' is nearly always plural. It's just about true that you don't have to go to church to be a Christian, but the New Testament assumes that the normal thing to do is to live out our faith in community with other Christians. We live in a low-commitment culture, whether it's in personal relationships or in social institutions like community groups, clubs and political parties, and studies of present-day Christianity have commented frequently on the phenomenon of 'believing without belonging'. Whether it's in what we would traditionally call a church, or whether it's a group in someone's home, or whether it's some kind of new monastic community life, we need to be with other Christians. That's the first level of our commitment to unity.

The next level is a commitment to unity between Christians. The exciting thing about learning from the Celtic Christians is that, as I explained in chapter two, they held together the different strands of Christianity which have now become divided, and in some cases institutionalised, into a multitude of denominations. Unity is not the same as uniformity. We don't need to find some way of coming together structurally across the globe, but what we do need to do is to recognise and affirm each other even when we differ. For some years, I was involved in an annual united act of worship with a local Roman Catholic church. In Christian unity week we would shut our Sunday service and go to the Catholic church to worship with them. When it came to Communion, we would move into a side room to share bread and wine as Anglicans, because officially we could not do so as part of the Mass. People in both churches found this awkward and painful, but it made the point that we were trying to stand as close together as possible while respecting the unresolved differences which still exist. It left most people wondering why, when Jesus told us to be united and to share bread and wine in memory of him, we still keep finding reasons not to. It's a good question.

The incredible diversity of the Christian church is something to enjoy, because it reflects the incredible diversity of human beings. We all have preferences about styles of worship because we are all different, but in the end they are just preferences. What we don't have the right to do is to insist that others must conform to what we like. Part of my application of this Way of Life is a commitment to try to connect with God in whatever kind of church I find myself and to try to enter in as fully as possible to what they are doing. That's sometimes a struggle when I help out at a nearby Anglo-Catholic church, because I can't stand the smell of incense close up. I've explained to them that, if they see my face wrinkled up, it's physical discomfort not theological disapproval! I genuinely enjoy the integrity and devotion of their rituals and ceremony where everything has a meaning and it's all to honour God.

Unity is challenging, especially at the moment. I can't ignore the fact that the church worldwide is deeply and painfully divided over issues of sexuality and gender but, because I follow a Way of Life with a stated commitment to the pursuit of unity, I'd like to offer some thoughts on this which may be helpful as we try to move forward.

For some Christians this issue is absolutely simple. Whenever the Bible mentions homosexual or lesbian sex it condemns it, and therefore to act on same-sex attraction is always wrong and we have to live sacrificially with the costly personal and pastoral consequences of abstinence. There is, however, another view, which observes that the interpretation of the relevant passages is, on closer examination, not simple, and it is possible that in each case the kinds of same-sex encounters they refer to are specific to their setting, and totally unlike the kinds of faithful, monogamous relationships we see today. The debate continues, but what is vital to observe is that on both sides are people who take the Bible very seriously as a guide to belief and behaviour, and who absolutely and genuinely wish to be faithful disciples of Jesus Christ. This fact alone should make us pause before rushing to judgement. It has always been a principle of biblical interpretation that what is complicated should be interpreted in the light of what is plain, and on this issue I think we need to step back and remind ourselves of some other things that scripture makes very plain.

There was a deep division in the New Testament church over the issue of whether non-Jews who became Christians had to take on all the Jewish practices of the first disciples, who were all Jews. This included adult male circumcision, which was an eye-wateringly unpopular act of commitment. One of the most important things Paul did was to set out at length and in great detail why the only thing necessary for being identified as a Christian was faith in Jesus Christ and nothing else: 'If you confess with your lips that Jesus is Lord and believe in your heart that God raised him from the dead, you will be saved' (Romans 10:9). Paul allowed that you could keep the Jewish law if you wanted to, but what you were not allowed to do was to force others to keep it (e.g. the discussion of food laws in Romans 14:1–9). The radical consequence of this is that we absolutely must without reservation accept as brothers and sisters in Christ everyone who has faith in him, even if, in good conscience, they come to different conclusions about how to live their life in a God-honouring way. Some lesbian and gay Christians will believe that God calls them to celibacy, while others believe that God will bless the faithful same-sex marriages they enter into.[52] We may never agree on this, but what is far more important is that we learn how to affirm one another and, as Paul says towards the end of his argument for unity, 'welcome one another, therefore, just as

Christ has welcomed you' (Romans 15:7). I honestly don't know how we are going to work this out in respect of church organisation and practice, but I believe that what matters more is that we start from the right place and understand what is of greatest importance. Some people say that we have got to allow ourselves to be led by love and stop arguing over what we think truth is. I think we should actually proceed the opposite way round. When we grasp the truth of what the Bible says about the basis of our unity in Christ, it enlarges our ability to love those with whom we disagree.

Unity and solidarity do not end, literally or metaphorically, at the church door. They are a vital part of how we relate to the people we meet in our day-to-day lives. One of the reasons why solving our divisions over sexuality and gender is so urgent is the impression of Christianity it gives to the world. One Sunday morning a friend was walking along the sea front in Brighton, a town which has always had a strong LGBTQIA+ community. He was wearing his clerical collar. He passed two young women sitting together on a bench, obviously a couple. As he passed, one of them looked up at him and simply asked, 'Why do you hate us so much?' That's a frightening wake-up call to the assumptions people make about Christians, and they are not groundless. I'm currently reading the autobiography of Laura Jane Grace, the transgender singer-guitarist of Against Me!, an American punk band. She describes her turbulent teenage years and a period of self-harm during which her family church sent her to a psychiatrist but also told her not to come back until she had received help. She writes, 'When a church turns you away, it feels as though God himself is rejecting you, saying you are damaged beyond his help.'[53] Not surprisingly, there's a strong anti-religious theme in some of their songs, but what I also hear is a tremendous passion and compassion for others going through similar emotional upheavals. Again, this is where different parts of this Way of Life weave together. We are committed to healing hurts and reconciling the divided. That begins by being open to the Spirit and listening. The greatest gift we can give to another person is to hear their story without prejudice.

Listening is also the key to our relationships with people of other faiths. As far as I can remember, every person in the village where I grew up and in the school I attended was white. Now, in the city where I live, it's easy to feel as if you are the only person speaking English when you travel on a bus or a train. The population of my neighbourhood is now 20 per cent Muslim, a proportion which has doubled in the last ten years. Too many Christians react to changes like this with fear. Some join in the complaints that they are being 'swamped' by migrants and refugees. Others feel that the remnants of Christianity will be swept away and that other faiths should not be allowed equal freedoms. Others who don't share these more repressive views still feel intimidated by the difficulty of sharing their faith with people who sometimes appear to be more outwardly devoted than we are.

Once again, our Way of Life comes to our aid. Our commitment to learning will lead us to the realisation that Christianity grew in an environment where every single person who heard the message of Jesus was already practising another religion of some kind, yet that did not hinder God. Next, we can draw again on our commitment to listening. If we show an interest in other people's faiths, they are often very willing to take an interest in ours. Recently my Muslim neighbours wanted to ask me about something. The woman spoke to my wife and asked me to call round. I have learned the Arabic Muslim greeting, 'As-salamu alaykum' (peace be upon you) and used it as soon as the door opened. The woman was so overjoyed that she shouted to her husband, 'He greeted us,' and immediately invited me in. They could not get over being offered a Muslim greeting by a Christian. I have discovered that, wherever we can find points of contact with people of other faiths, it leads easily and comfortably to questions and conversations about the things over which we differ. Not only does that allow us to share Christ, but also it is another step towards building tolerance and defusing tension in our prejudice-torn world.

As we'll see in the next chapter, meeting people where they are is a vital part of evangelism. At a deeper level, though, recognising our common humanity is an essential part of discipleship. As we saw in the opening chapters, to grow as a Christian, to be a disciple of Christ, is ultimately about becoming more fully human. Part of that process is learning to see that which is of God in every other human being, no matter how different from us they may be. This waymark is about changing our thinking and changing the way we act. As we do so, it will open up as never before the glorious diversity of God's human creations and, as we find new solidarity with others, so we will find ever more to celebrate together.

To think about:

- What does being part of a Christian church or group mean to you?

- Which Christian stream, or style of worship, do you feel least at home with, and how could you expand your horizons?

For a group:

- Discuss which groups of people we feel are most different to us, and how we might build bridges towards them.

12

Waymark ten:
share Jesus and justice

The last command Jesus gave to his followers was to 'make disciples of all nations' (Matthew 28:19–20) as the final stage of God's 'plan for the fullness of time, to gather up all things in Christ, things in heaven and things on earth' (Ephesians 1:10). The reason we are called to live in united community is 'that the world may believe' (John 17:21). An essential goal of our Way of Life, therefore, is to develop a disciplined spirituality which will make us effective witnesses for Christ. Centres of Christian community like Iona and Lindisfarne were mission bases for the spread of the gospel in the British Isles. Leaders like Aidan, Hilda, Cuthbert, Columba, David and Patrick made Christ known to others through words and actions wherever they went. They shared the gospel in ways which respected and began from the existing culture and beliefs of their hearers.

All Christians are empowered by the Holy Spirit to be witnesses (Acts 1:8), so, motivated by the love of Christ (2 Corinthians 5:14), we seek to share our faith wherever God gives us an opportunity, taking time to listen to others before we speak. We seek to be led by the Spirit into new ways of sharing Christ which fit the culture in which we live, and to be open to demonstrations of the Spirit's power through prayer for healing and prophetic insights.

By speaking the truth prayerfully and in love we also seek to introduce God's peaceful rule wherever material or spiritual powers have taken his place. Following the example of Jesus, we also seek to minister to, and speak for, those oppressed by poverty and injustice (Matthew 11:2–5). The Celtic missionaries actively sought to bring a Christian influence to bear upon people in power to cause them to act justly and to open wider doors for the gospel. We seek to work with all people of goodwill in positions of influence so that our nations may reflect the values of the kingdom of God.

When someone becomes a member of the Community of Aidan and Hilda, we hold a special service called the First Voyage of the Coracle, inspired by the Celtic image of setting out on a Spirit-led journey for the love of God, at which they make their commitment to follow the Community's Way of Life. As a Guardian of the Community I often lead these services. I get to speak the following words, which have never failed to capture my imagination since I first heard them at someone else's First Voyage:

God is giving you a vision of a spoiled creation being restored to harmony with its creator, of a fragmented world being made whole, of a weakened church being restored to its mission, of lands being healed and lit up by the glorious Trinity.

As anyone who knows me well will testify, I am not a morning person, but this is a vison worth getting out of bed for!

I have never needed any persuading about the importance of sharing Jesus with others – or, to give it its biblical name, evangelism – because without evangelism I would not be a Christian. I did not grow up in a family that went to church and, although the local vicar came and did school assemblies, he just told funny little stories which made no sense to me at all. It all changed one day in my teens when I used 'Jesus

Christ' as a swear word once too often and a friend of mine told me to stop it. I asked him why it mattered and he outed himself as a Christian. That started a long process of questions and arguments with him and several other friends, who put up with my sarcasm and scepticism and kept on answering my questions and objections. I discovered what no one had ever told me before: that it was possible to connect with God in an ongoing and deepening relationship. Once I discovered that, it was obvious to me that this was the most important and relevant thing in the world and, even though I didn't know how to do it, I wanted to play my part in letting others know. One of the things which drew me to the Community of Aidan and Hilda was that it offered a way for me to keep the fire of the Spirit alive amid the pressures of life and ministry, and held out this inspiring integrated vision not just of people reconciled with God, but of all creation healed and restored. Since it was the Celtic saints who first lit up the Dark Ages, what better root could there be with which to reconnect?

This, as I have long known, is not obvious to all Christians. Many of us find the idea of evangelism deeply uncomfortable, not only because we are often unsure about how to go about it, but also because we feel, as Becky Pippert famously put it, that 'evangelism was something you shouldn't do to your dog, let alone a friend'.[54] Part of the problem may be the way that Jesus' Great Commission (Matthew 28:16–20) gets translated into English. In New Testament Greek, all you need to do to change the word 'disciple' into a word meaning 'what-has-to-happen-for-someone-to-become-a-disciple' is to change a few letters. In English we have to add a whole new word so we end up with the phrase 'make disciples', which sounds horribly like compelling people to do something they don't want to do. Similarly, the word 'evangelism', or 'to evangelise', simply means to tell someone something which is good news. While there is a place for discussion, debate and dealing with objections to what we believe, at its most basic level evangelism is simply sharing the good news that, through Jesus dying and rising from the dead, God is mending our broken world.[55] Within the setting of this good news, some of the old ABC ways of explaining how to become a Christian come back to life. In response to the God who made us and loves us, we need to *accept* that we have fallen short of God's best for our lives, *believe* that through Jesus we are forgiven and reconciled to God and *commit* ourselves to following him.

You may have noticed that this simple presentation of the Christian message makes no mention of hell and judgement. Before anyone gets concerned, let me be quite clear that the Bible in general, and Jesus in particular, says a great deal about God's judgement upon all that is evil. What makes some of us feel very uneasy is the way in which this is often used as a motivation for evangelism. Leaving aside the important question of just what is meant by the word we translate as 'hell', it is still the case that for many centuries the Christian message has often been, in effect, 'Come to Jesus for forgiveness or something very bad will happen to you when you die'. That sounds to some of us like a sinister threat poorly disguised as good news and we feel uneasy about it. Again, I am not wanting in any way to compromise the reality that 'all have sinned and fall short of the glory of God' (Romans 3:23) and that 'the wages of sin is death' (Romans 6:23), or that the message of forgiveness through Jesus' death on the cross is not wonderfully liberating for people who need to be set free from their past. What I have come to realise is that, in the missionary C.T. Studd's famous phrase, the main motivation for Paul and the other apostles was not 'to run a rescue shop within a yard of hell'.

Paul tells us what keeps him going as a missionary, sharing Christ in town after town and sometimes enduring physical violence for doing so: 'The love of Christ urges us on, because we are convinced that one has died for all… From now on, therefore, we regard no one from a human point of view' (2 Corinthians 5:14–16). What motivates Paul is love, a profound gratitude for what God in Christ has done for him, a profound grasp of what this means for the whole world and a profound compassion for others, which means he will do all that he can to give them a chance to know God as he has come to know him. 'Love never ends,' as he writes elsewhere (1 Corinthians 13:8). It is love which motivates us to share Jesus and 'perfect love casts out fear' (1 John 4:18). An earlier waymark encourages us to be open to the Spirit. It is the Spirit who empowers us to be witnesses (Acts 1:8) and who enables us to be fired by love and not by fear. A missionary, as British evangelist J. John puts it, isn't someone who crosses the sea but someone who sees the cross. Ask God to help you to see others as he sees them.

Our ability to share our faith is nothing to do with our personality. So often we get the impression that the most effective witnesses are articulate extroverts who can talk the back legs off a donkey. Quiet, gentle people who listen to others and tirelessly show kindness can make just as much of a positive impact when people ask them where they get their patience from. God can and will use each one of us, and the different elements of this Way of Life help us to become more effective sharers of good news.

Evangelism begins in prayer as, in our daily prayer rhythms, we pray for God's just and merciful rule to grow on earth. It's worth remembering that even Paul asked people to pray for him that 'God will open to us a door for the word' (Colossians 4:3), and for boldness in taking the opportunities when they came (Ephesians 6:19–20). Prayer like this takes all the stress out of sharing our faith because we are asking God to give us the right moment to speak, which we can reasonably assume means when the person listening is open to hearing.

Our commitment to unity and to listening means that we will get alongside people where they are and try to understand them before we try to tell them things. One of the features of St Aidan's missionary work in seventh-century Northumbria was that he refused to ride a horse so that he was always on the same level as the ordinary people and could talk to them wherever he went. Getting alongside people where they are and as they are is vital. Whitby, where St Hilda had her great Celtic community, is now a centre for goths, inspired by its connection with Bram Stoker's *Dracula*. People in amazing clothes, jet jewellery and dark make-up gather among the gravestones in the ancient churchyard. One of the sisters from the local convent often goes out to offer them bottles of water. She says her dark robes and veil make her fit in well! I will never forget hearing someone in the church I attended while at university being interviewed about how she came to faith. She turned to the person standing at the front with her and said, 'Your friendship was the bridge over which Jesus walked into my life.'

Lifelong learning means we will always try to get better at explaining our faith and finding answers to the questions people ask us. Remember 'I don't know but I'll find out' is a perfectly good way of dealing with a tough question. Yet on a simpler level our perspective of life as journeying with God means that we will have reflected on our own spiritual journey. The simplest way of sharing the good news is telling our own faith story. Yours may not be at all like mine, with a specific moment when you became a Christian. If you grew up in a Christian family, you will still be able to talk about how your faith became real and personal to you. The one thing on which we are all an expert is our own life story and, even if someone else does not come to share our beliefs, they can never deny the reality to us of our experience. Last, our openness to the Spirit will make us increasingly sensitive to the times when it is right to speak and the times when we just need to listen.

Mission is not just about Jesus; it's also about justice. When Jesus spoke about setting the captives free, he was not just speaking in a spiritual sense. In the ancient world, Christianity looked unattractive. It originated among the Jews, who were seen as troublemakers, it centred on a man who was crucified and it challenged most conventional ideas of religious practice. One of the reasons this unlikely faith caught on was the behaviour of its followers. Julian, the last pagan Roman emperor, wrote in the fourth century that one reason why it was hard to persuade people not to become Christians was that they 'support not only their own poor but ours as well'.[56] In the seventh century, Aidan used money given to the Lindisfarne community to go and buy slaves, whom he then set free. In the 18th century, John Wesley travelled the country preaching several times a day most days, but also spent many hours in between collecting money and organising schools to relieve the appalling poverty of working people. I think it was Martin Luther King who said that it is not enough to save people's souls from hell if we allow them to continue living in it from day to day.

The need to work against poverty and injustice is obvious from the life and teaching of Jesus, who challenged the people of his day to love not just their Jewish neighbours but also their pagan enemies. In Great Britain, Christians were deeply involved from the start in the provision of education and health care, the abolition of slavery and the establishment of fair working conditions. Christians today are highly involved in things like the campaign against human trafficking,[57] or working to raise people out of poverty through initiatives like food banks.

Yet many of these issues require more than charity to solve them. Instead, the very structures of society need changing. Many Christians share the cynicism of wider society about politics, or feel that this is not something in which they should be involved. We are beginning to regain an understanding that, because of the intertwining of what we call religion and politics, nearly everything that Jesus said or did was politically explosive, and when Paul went into the Roman Empire announcing 'good news', he was using the same expression that Roman emperors used to tell everyone how good their regime was. By describing Jesus as Lord and Saviour, Paul was using titles which some of the emperors used. Jesus and Paul were not persecuted for telling people to love each other but because what they said indirectly or directly called into question the ruling powers.

Both Jesus and Paul lived in an empire where power was tightly held by a few people and where just about the only way to bring about change was violent revolution, which Christianity directly opposed. For that reason, the New Testament seems to say little about politics as we understand it. Nevertheless, Paul sees even imperial governmental structures as being God-given (Romans 13:1–7) and Jeremiah encourages the exiles in Babylon to 'seek the welfare of the city where I have sent you' (Jeremiah 29:7). The stories about Daniel and his friends portray Jews getting highly involved in the government of a pagan empire and having to negotiate the difficult decisions about when and when not to compromise their distinctiveness. As part of this Way of Life, we should at the very least be politically informed as part of our involvement in society, and open to getting involved in governmental and political structures where appropriate. Despite the fact that, unlike in the United States, it is deeply unfashionable to be known to have religious beliefs if you are a politician, many of our politicians have been very open about their faith. Keir Hardie, founder of the Labour Party, frequently said that 'the impetus which drove me first into the Labour movement, and the inspiration which has carried me on in it, has been derived more from the teachings of Jesus of Nazareth than from all other sources combined'.[58] Most of the mainstream British political parties have Christian groups within them, trying in different ways to work out the values of the kingdom. Getting involved can be messy and challenging, but getting our hands dirty to make other people's lives better is precisely what following Jesus is all about.

To think about:

- Think about your personal faith journey. Imagine explaining it simply to someone who is not a Christian.

- Make your own prayer list of between three and seven people you know who are not yet Christians, and start to pray for them.

For a group:

- Share ideas of what a society based on the priorities and practices of Jesus would be like. Where do you see these things happening in society and government today, and where are they lacking?

13

Three life-giving principles

I believe that living by a Way of Life is a vital ancient practice which modern Christians need to rediscover because it gives us a sustainable and lifelong way to become mature followers and imitators of Jesus. No Way of Life is absolutely perfect or complete, of course, which is why different Christian communities have come up with different versions, which often also reflect their own particular emphases. Hopefully, though, you can see that the often interconnected waymarks we've explored in the last ten chapters cover a pretty broad spread of what it takes to connect more deeply with God and connect God with the whole of life. Certainly, it's been my own experience, and that of many people I know, that this is precisely what happens when you follow this practice.

The early Christian communities were also quite diverse, as their Ways, or Rules, of Life illustrate. Some of these are very specific about how the life of a close community is to be ordered, while others focus on wider qualities of character. We often think of these communities as very austere but sometimes they are refreshingly down to earth. For example, the Rule of Ciaran contains this warning: 'Wise rules do not conceal the fact that praising their own actions while belittling the efforts of others is a very common fault among clerics'.[59] The most famous Rule is that of St Benedict, which has shaped the life of many monastic communities up to the present day.[60]

The three most well-known commitments made by members of monastic communities are poverty, chastity and obedience, made popular by St Francis of Assisi in the early 13th century, and sometimes known as the 'Evangelical [i.e. based on the gospels] Counsels'. These vows make perfect sense in highly organised communities made up of people committed to a life of singleness,[61] sharing all property in common, and growing or making everything they need. However, that is not how most of us live, and if the idea of living by a Way of Life is actually something beneficial for all Christians, then these three commitments need to be expressed in a new way to fit the lives of people who often live in families and have a regular job outside their home. For this reason, this Way of Life, based on that of the Community of Aidan and Hilda and following the example of some other new monastic communities, reinterprets these vows as three life-giving principles, which we call *simplicity*, *purity* and *obedience*. Normally these would be set out before the ten waymarks because they run like a thread through all of them, but on reflection it seemed to me that they are better understood once you have seen all the waymarks and have a clearer idea of what is involved in this Way of Life. Let's examine them one by one.

Simplicity

Jesus said: 'Strive first for the kingdom of God and his righteousness, and all these things [food and clothing] will be given to you as well' (Matthew 6:33). The essence of simplicity is to put the priorities and values of God's kingdom first in every area of life. This leads us to regard all that we have as gifts not as possessions, to be used as God guides us, and to trust that God will provide for our essential needs.

One of the things I love about days in the mountains is that they are essentially very simple. There is a summit to be reached or a ridge to be traversed, and everything else works together to that end. All your skills and experience are in play (including knowing when to back off), you take only the equipment which is fit for purpose, and in a team you rely on one another. On the best days, you are utterly absorbed in what you are doing, whether it's having every sense alert navigating in the mist on the Cairngorm plateau, or concentrating on climbing moves on a winter traverse of Glen Coe's spiky Aonach Eagach ridge. Coming back to London is always plunging head first back into complexity, with an inbox full of emails, calls on the answer phone, people to see and an array of tasks to be completed every week. Choice overload is one of the burdens of 21st-century living. Apparently, many supermarkets stock 100 types of breakfast cereal. No wonder we feel tired all the time! A Way of Life provides a path through this jungle, because it makes clear from the beginning what our top priority is: 'strive first for the kingdom of God' (Matthew 6:33), or, to put it another way, one with which we might now be familiar, connect more deeply with God and connect God with the whole of life.

Soon after I became a Christian, I was taught that the way to order life is to put God first, family second and everything else third. Basic as it sounds, I still think that's right. It's so tempting to put work, career or even Christian ministry ahead of the people and the person who matter most. The way to avoid it is – to state the obvious – to put into our personal application of this Way of Life how we are going to put our connection with God first in our daily rhythms, and where we are going to guarantee time for our families or significant other people in our lives. Putting the priorities and values of God's kingdom first in every area of our lives will mean that we will want to seek his guidance (and discuss with our Soul Friend) significant decisions such as our work choices and progression, our use of money, where we live, and perhaps our personal relationships. I am so glad that when I became a Christian it was made very clear to me that, in the jargon of the time, accepting Jesus as Saviour meant accepting Jesus as Lord. I remember wondering what would happen if God told me to give all my money away, only to be wisely advised that he doesn't do that for most people, if he does he will make it very clear and also provide in other ways, and in any case all our money belongs to him but most of the time he lets us keep most of it! It left me in no doubt that becoming a Christian was a serious commitment, which would change the overall direction of my life. If you know that, it becomes easier to make other decisions.

If we regard seeking God's best for our lives as our top priority, and see everything we have as his gift, then another outworking of simplicity is exploring the gift of ourselves. All of us have God-given gifts, activated by the Holy Spirit, and identifying and learning to use them is a vital part of determining what God is calling us to do in our lives.[62] A further stage is to explore the God-given distinctives of our own personalities, using processes like Myers–Briggs profiling or the more complex and nuanced Enneagram process.[63] Understanding ourselves reduces conflict with other people because we understand why they are different, and helps us to work with the grain of who we are rather than fighting ourselves. The result in both cases is a simpler and more harmonious life, keeping in step with the rhythm of the Spirit.

Purity

Jesus said: 'Blessed are the pure in heart, for they will see God' (Matthew 5:8). The essence of purity is being open before God in all our thoughts and feelings, including our sexuality. We show love, openness and generosity to all people following the example of Christ, but reserve the sexual expression of love for a lifelong partner. We honour marriage, respect those who choose to remain single, and affirm those for whom this area of life is a struggle.

This is the only place in the Way of Life that speaks specifically about our sexuality, although I talked about some of our struggles in this area of life in chapter eleven. In fact, sexual purity is only one aspect of this principle, and probably not the most important one.

We need to talk about sex because the rest of the western world does so constantly, and also because the Bible talks about it. In the ancient world, religion and morality were two different things. You went to the temple to do your duty to the gods and you talked with the philosophers about how to live. When it came to sex, the Greek statesman Demosthenes summed it up in one sentence: 'We have mistresses for our enjoyment, concubines to serve our needs and wives to bear legitimate children.' Jews and Christians were unusual in that they insisted that what we do with our bodies is as important in our relationship with God as what we do in prayer. It's very easy to read into the Bible whatever we think is normal and then use the scriptures to justify what we think. With regard to sex, we need to be aware that the idea of purity had a lot to do with what was considered to be 'the done thing', and that marriage had a lot to do with personal property and possession.[64] That said, the Bible does give us clear guidelines for how to behave sexually. Faithfulness to our partner and not exploiting others are the supreme values (see 1 Thessalonians 4:3–8 and Matthew 5:27–28), and marriage is meant to be for life.

For obvious reasons, our sexuality is a deeply sensitive part of who we are and too often Christianity has addressed this in a way that is condemnatory and shaming. This is not the way of Jesus. We see his bold compassion towards a woman accused of adultery (John 8:1–11), and the writer to the Hebrews tells us that, in Jesus,

> We do not have a high priest who is unable to sympathise with our weaknesses, but we have one who in every respect has been tested as we are, yet without sin. Let us therefore approach the throne of grace with boldness, so that we may receive mercy and find grace to help in time of need.
> HEBREWS 4:15–16

This brings us to what purity is really about. 'Blessed are the pure in heart,' said Jesus, 'for they will see God' (Matthew 5:8). In the modern world view, we think in our heads and feel in our hearts, but in the world of the Bible you think in your heart and feel in your guts. Nevertheless, there is still a close connection between the two because what we think has a huge influence upon what we feel. Purity in this context therefore speaks of a transparency before God about what is going on in our minds and hearts, a transparency that is possible because we have nothing to fear from God, who knows us perfectly but does not condemn us for what is imperfect. One of the key practices in desert and Celtic spirituality was to be absolutely open with God (and with a Soul Friend, although this will require time for trust to reach a level where many of us will feel fully able to do this) about what was going on in the mind – good and bad. That openness in the face of God's love relieves shame and self-condemnation, reduces our anger at ourselves, which often expresses itself as anger at the faults of others and opens us up to a greater sympathy towards their faults. The practice of silence, which we explored in an earlier chapter, is vital in building this transparency with God, and as we practise it regularly we find our inner world becoming purified as the clutter in our heads begins to settle and we start to be able to see God, who was there all along, more clearly. The Celtic Christians spoke about 'the single eye', picking up Jesus' image of the eye as the lamp of the body (Matthew 6:22–23). The more we achieve this purity of vision, the sharper our focus becomes on the waymarks of our Way of Life, the deeper our connection with God and the connection with God in each part of our lives.

Obedience

> Jesus said: 'Those who want to save their life will lose it, and those who lose their life for my sake will find it' (Matthew 16:25). The essence of obedience is the joyful abandonment of ourselves to God, giving up our will for his in the service of others. The root of obedience is therefore in learning to listen to God to learn his ways. We also give due respect to those whom God has placed in positions of leadership or seniority in church, family, the workplace and public life.

Obedience is not a comfortable idea for many of us because we live in a culture of disrespect for authority, often rooted in feelings of having been let down by people in positions of responsibility. This is an area of life in which we are called to be seriously countercultural: 'Pay to all what is due them – taxes to whom taxes are due, revenue to whom revenue is due, respect to whom respect is due, honour to whom honour is due' (Romans 13:7). As a church minister, my work in the local community often brings me into contact with local politicians, either councillors or Members of Parliament from various parties. There are of course exceptions, but I have rarely come across a politician, local or national, who did not seem to genuinely believe that they were seeking the good of all, and all of them work very hard. That doesn't mean that in a democracy we do not also offer criticism where criticism is due, but we do so with respect. A few years ago, we hosted a civic service for the mayor and all the councillors. At the end, I invited the congregation to applaud them all for their work in our community. Some of the councillors were genuinely moved by this because they are so rarely thanked and shown appreciation.

The same can often apply to church leaders. Paul urges the Thessalonians to 'respect those who labour among you… esteem them very highly in love because of their work' (1 Thessalonians 5:12–13). Sadly, there are some church leaders who seem to be too interested in power and their own ego, but most are genuinely trying to do their best for God and the people in their care. As I talk to members of other churches, I sometimes hear complaints about things their leaders are doing (or not doing). I normally ask if they've spoken about it with the person in question. The answer is nearly always no, and that shows a lack of respect; we are criticising someone behind their back without giving them a chance to improve.

The one to whom we owe ultimate obedience is God. One of the things that amazes me about God is the extent of his patience. Sometimes we read the Old Testament as a book of wrath and judgement. It's astonishing to realise that when the kingdoms of Israel and Judah were constantly turning away from God back to pagan worship, ignoring his commandments and creating a society in which the rich exploited the poor, and even on occasions practising human sacrifice, God sent prophet after prophet to urge them to turn back to him and in the end allowed more than a century to pass before finally withdrawing his protection from their nation and allowing them to suffer the consequences of their action. God is the ultimate authority and he is utterly committed to our well-being. What he asks us to do is for our good.

The word 'obedience' is intimately linked to the idea of listening. As Abbot Christopher Jamison explains:

> 'Obedience' derives from the Latin word *oboedire*, which means not only 'to obey' but also 'to listen'. The prefix *ob-* means 'in the direction of', added to *audire*, 'to hear', which becomes *oboedire*. So obedience conjures up an image of leaning towards somebody, straining to hear what they are saying.[65]

This takes us right to the heart of grasping that being a Christian is not about following a set of rules but cultivating a relationship. As we seek to put this Way of Life into practice, the most essential skill is to learn to listen to God so that we can learn from him how each of these waymarks is to be applied and lived out in our own personal and unique circumstances.

To think about:

- How easy do you find it to be open with God about all your thoughts and feelings?

- If the idea at the root of obedience is that of attentive listening, how can you be more intentional about how you listen to God?

For a group:

- What do we think Jesus means for us today when he says, 'Seek first the kingdom of God', and where do we find this most challenging?

14

Getting started

How are you feeling – excited, inspired, exhausted, overwhelmed, bewildered? If it's any or all of these, don't worry; you're not the first one. One of the most common reactions to reading through a Way of Life like this one is to feel utterly daunted by the enormity of what looks to be the task ahead. The first question is usually something like: 'This looks great but how on earth am I going to do all this?'

Here's the good news: a Way of Life isn't called a Way of Life for nothing. In the first place, you don't have to do it all at once. In fact, you've got the rest of your life to work out what all this means, because this is a map for a lifelong journey. What's more, a Way of Life is meant to be a way that gives life. It's a response to the grace of the God who is already with us and in us by his Spirit, rather than a ladder of good works designed to bring us close to a God who is far from us. Ken Shigematsu is a Canadian evangelical pastor whose family originates from Japan. While researching his family tree, he discovered that some of his ancestors were Samurai, whose code of life, *bushido*, embraced not just warfare but growing in wisdom to equip them for every walk of life. Ken wondered how he could find something like that for Christians, and on a visit to Ireland he discovered Celtic spirituality. He gives one of the best explanations of what a Way of Life is all about: 'A rule of life is simply a rhythm of practices that empowers us to live well and grow more like Jesus by helping us experience the presence of God in everything.'[66] He continues: 'The word "rule" comes from a Greek word that means "trellis". A trellis is a support system for a vine or plant that enables it to grow upward and bear fruit... Grapevines in the wild will use just about anything – a tree or even a rock – as a trellis. It is part of their nature to seek structure. Like a trellis, a rule of life supports and guides our growth.'[67] What matters is our life in God. That's the living plant. Our Way of Life is the supporting structure that helps it to grow.

How then do we start to build our trellis? Several times along the way, I have made the point that no Way of Life is a perfect embodiment of everything that Christianity is all about. There are many, many different kinds of Christian communities that live by a Way of Life. You'll find that they have lots of things in common but also their own distinctive emphases.[68] A Way of Life is often caught, not taught. I was already on a search for something more when I discovered the Community of Aidan and Hilda. Celtic spirituality seemed to hold together in one place so many things that I was looking for that it was an obvious step to join the Community and start following its Way of Life. When I became convinced that God was prompting me to introduce a Way of Life at the Church of the Ascension, I followed what I believe was the model of the Celtic Christians. When Aidan went to Lindisfarne, he was sent and trained by Columba's community on Iona. The very fact that Aidan founded his community on an island shows how deeply steeped he was in Columba's ways, so I have no doubt that the Way of Life he followed would have been the Rule of Columba. Yet the reason Aidan went was that a previous mission had failed because its approach was too rigid. Aidan was adaptable, so I am sure he would have made alterations to Columba's Way of Life to fit his new circumstances, not least being in a Saxon warrior culture rather than an Irish monastery. Aidan then mentored Hilda, who later led the great community at Whitby. I have no doubt that what Hilda taught would probably have been called the Rule of Aidan, but again she was a wise and sensitive leader of great stature so I suspect she would also have made changes as she saw fit, and I cannot imagine anyone who had been to Whitby coming away thinking they had been living anything other than the Rule of Hilda.

For that reason, while the Way of Life presented in this book is closely based on that of the Community of Aidan and Hilda, it is not identical. I rewrote it partly to put it into a style and voice that people in my church were used to hearing, and also to bring in some emphases and insights which I felt were important from my experience in a local church. You might want to look around and explore other Ways of Life from other communities. If that leads you to find the one that fits you best, then go ahead and adopt it and maybe join that community if appropriate. However, I am passing on what I know and have lived for nearly 20 years, so why not try out what you have found in this book? You might at some stage want to alter it or maybe to change some of the specific waymarks, but my very strong advice would be to try it as it is for at least a year to see how it feels in practice.

Yes, I did say at least a year! As I said above, the good news about this Way of Life is that you do not have to do everything at once. Equally, it goes against most of our contemporary expectations in that there is nothing instant about it. For this to be properly life-giving as it is meant to be, it needs time.

The three life-giving principles and the ten waymarks are universal, that is to say they apply to everyone everywhere, but how they apply may differ wildly from one person to another. Therefore, the first step in starting to live by this Way of Life is to work out your personal application of it. Here is more good news: you are probably already doing quite a lot of it already.

Here is a simple exercise I often use when introducing the idea of living by a Way of Life. Spend a short period of time (you can do this in 10–15 minutes, but up to about half an hour would be better) jotting down your answers to the following questions:

1 How am I seeking to grow in knowledge?
2 How do I experience companionship on my spiritual journey?
3 What is my personal rhythm of prayer, work and rest?

4   What are my guiding principles in my use of money and possessions?

5   What steps do I take to care for the environment?

6   How do I help others find healing?

7   What do I do to enable the Holy Spirit to guide me?

8   How do I support others through prayer?

9   How do I show welcome and hospitality to other people?

10 How do I help others to find faith in Jesus?

Each of these questions is drawn from one of the waymarks. They don't by any means embody the whole of what each waymark is all about, but they do provide a starting point. Most people find they can write at least one thing down for at least seven or eight of these questions, and when you look at what you've written you will find that you already have a basic Way of Life. You may just never have thought of it like that before!

With that encouragement, it's now time to go deeper and explore each waymark in more depth. What I've attempted to do in this book is to describe each waymark and then explain it in greater detail with some suggestions about what it may look like in practice. I am deeply indebted to my friend Ray Simpson, Founding Guardian of the Community of Aidan and Hilda, and one of the authors of its original Way of Life. Ray's book *New Celtic Monasticism For Everyday People*,[69] first published under the much better title of *A Pilgrim Way*, not only tells the story of the Community but provides a full commentary on its Way of Life. Ray's insights are different to my own, but in each chapter he provides examples of how different people apply each of the waymarks. You might find his book helpful to read alongside this one. When I first joined the Community, I spent the best part of a year praying and thinking about each waymark and gradually writing down how I felt it could be applied in my own life.

Part of the principle of simplicity is that our Way of Life should be clear and achievable. John Maxwell, who has written extensively on the subject of leadership, likes to say that if you want to change your life you need to change something you do every day. That's wise advice. Part of my rhythm of prayer, work and recreation is to exercise regularly. That's a good thing to do as part of looking after our bodies, but for me there's also the incentive that London is a long way from the nearest mountain and, when I do get there, I want to avoid the utter misery of plodding uphill gasping and sweating because I am unfit. That doesn't mean I like exercise, though! I know that if I wrote in my Way of Life that I will exercise regularly, that could easily mean I end up going for a run once a month, if I remember. So instead I have made a commitment to do some kind of high-energy exercise once a week – and writing this reminds me that I haven't done it this week! Try, therefore, to be as specific as possible about what you commit to do.

At the same time, do not take on too much. I was wisely warned by my first Soul Friend not to, as he put it, write a heroic list of things I would try to do and then fail to do them. That's why it's so important to start with what you're doing already, not least because you'll probably be pleasantly surprised by how much of this Way of Life you already follow to some degree. Having done that, you can then start to give attention to the gaps. I would suggest that for each waymark you do not try to add more than one thing that you are not already doing, and even then I would advise only trying to add at most three or four new things in total to your Way of Life in any given year. In some cases, you may find a waymark which has no expression at all in your life at present, and which may be full of things that are entirely new to you. Some of the stuff on healing is very new to some Christians, while others may never have given much thought to the environment in a Christian context. In these cases, you might want to make a commitment that in the next twelve months you will try and learn more about that waymark and then after that work out how you are going to apply it.

No one is meant to walk their journey with God alone, which is why this Way of Life includes the essential practice of Soul Friendship. When people join the Community of Aidan and Hilda, the first question they often ask is 'Can you help me find a Soul Friend?' There are several ways you can go about this. There might already be someone in your church or in a local network who has a ministry of what is called 'spiritual direction.' In chapter three of *Creating Community*, I explained the similarities and differences between spiritual direction and Soul Friendship. Essentially they are very similar. If you know someone with this ministry, then why not book in for a trial session? A second possibility is to see if there is a traditional religious community somewhere nearby. Many of these offer spiritual direction to guests who come there for a retreat or just to anyone who needs it, so you may find that a helpful place to enquire. Often people who have never stayed at a community imagine that monks and nuns are very unworldly and out of touch. You will be pleasantly surprised to find that they aren't and you'll often find a lot of humour too. Living with the same small group of people for years on end teaches you a lot about human nature, and also the need to laugh.

Many of us, however, may not have such contacts, but the answer may be nearer than we think. In *Creating Community*, I shared some very helpful advice on finding a Soul Friend, and I'll repeat it here.

First of all, think about, and maybe write down, what you would want from a Soul Friend. This might include:

- Help with praying or listening to God
- Help with working out and applying your Way of Life
- Help with spiritual growth and understanding
- Help with processing your emotions and inner life
- Help with making important decisions

Next, bear in mind the four basic qualities of a Soul Friend: listening skills, reflectiveness, prayerfulness and a personal dedication to trying to walk closely with God. It goes without saying that they should also be able to keep confidences.

Now think about what you would like your ideal Soul Friend to be like. This might include some of the following factors:

- Male or female?
- Older than you are?
- An ordained minister?
- A member of a religious community?
- Rooted within a particular Christian tradition; e.g. Roman Catholic, evangelical, Orthodox, charismatic, etc.?
- A trained spiritual director?
- Able to be contacted outside of scheduled meetings?
- Available by phone, email and/or online chat?
- Formal or informal in style?

Now make a list of everyone you know who might come close to meeting most or all of the criteria on your list. You may now have a shortlist of people you could approach to be a Soul Friend. Needless to say, they may not be familiar with this terminology, but you may be surprised how many Christians are open to being asked if, every few months, they would be willing to sit and listen to someone talk about how their journey with God is going. You may not find a Soul Friend immediately, but remember that Jesus made a promise about keeping on asking, knocking and seeking. It's worth it. I should however mention that while two people can be Soul Friends to one another, it is always important to be clear about who is talking and who is listening when you meet. Don't try and do both in one meeting because the person who is listening needs to keep a clear head, unclouded by their own concerns and agenda. Likewise, and I am frequently asked this, it is not good for your partner to be your Soul Friend. For one thing, it is almost impossible for them to keep enough detachment to listen clearly and, more importantly, it will be very difficult if the issue you want to talk about most is your partner! Just remember, though, you will find a Soul Friend somewhere.

In the final chapter of *Creating Community*, I wrote about how I went about introducing a Way of Life, a rhythm of prayer and the practice of Soul Friendship into my church in Ealing. If you're a church leader and already used to introducing new ideas, then hopefully what you've read already in this book will have given you plenty of ideas on how introduce a Way of Life into your own setting, but there are more in my first book. The only point I would emphasise is that this is something which needs to be practised before it is taught. Bede wrote of Aidan that 'he taught them no other way of life than that which he himself practised among his fellows'.[70] St Luke's Church in Johannesburg, South Africa, are seeking to adopt a Way of Life and to be able to provide a Soul Friend for anyone who wants one, particularly their young people. When I visited them in 2016, I was delighted to find that they had already started implementing the things I had written about, and as a first stage every member of the church leadership team had committed to meeting with a Soul Friend or spiritual director. They were making sure that they first practised what they intended to preach. Part of the vision of the Community of Aidan and Hilda is to help the wider church share the things we've rediscovered, and we're delighted to offer any help and support you may need to get started.

To think about

- The application for this chapter is simply to work through it. In a group you might want to share with each other how you are getting on.

Conclusion

In February 2017, for the first time in my life, I went on a protest march. Around the time that I marched, in the United States and many European countries, borders were being closed out of fear that we might be infiltrated by Islamic terrorists. Yet barely a year earlier we saw pictures of a dead Syrian child washed up on the shores of the Mediterranean as his family fled from the brutal civil war in their homeland. As the Somali-British poet Warsan Shire wrote, 'No one puts their children in a boat unless the water is safer than the land'.[71] Yet, out of fear, many of our countries were closing their doors to the poor, the strangers and the outcasts. Others may disagree, but for me as a Christian that cannot be right, and I cannot stand by and do nothing.

On that day, tens of thousands of people marched from the US Embassy to Downing Street chanting, 'Refugees are welcome here!' I was very moved by the whole occasion. Muslims proclaimed their desire to live in an open and inclusive society. Jewish representatives spoke in welcome of the Muslims. People who in many parts of the world are at each other's throats stood in solidarity with each other. As a member of the Community of Aidan and Hilda, I was wearing, as I nearly always do, a distinctive Celtic cross. Among all the other faiths standing together in compassionate solidarity, it was the only visible sign of a Christian presence that I saw all day. I wondered why. In the evening, I shared some pictures and my reflections on social media, some on a public page. Within an hour I had plenty of responses. I was called a supporter of terrorism, ignorant of the Bible and deceived by Satan, and was personally abused by people who had never met me. All of them said they were Christians.

This is why discipleship matters. Christian values of love, welcome, generosity and compassion have been the foundations which, in theory if not always in practice, have shaped the values of societies across the Western world and beyond. The reason those values were adopted was that people lived them out with enough integrity that others wanted to be like them, until eventually they became the shared values of whole countries. Christendom is over, and the values it created are being destroyed at a frightening pace, accelerated by people who call themselves Christians but seem to have little about them which speaks of good news.

There is a better way, the way of Jesus, but the post-Christian world will only see that when it is lived. 'People today don't read Bibles,' someone once told me, 'but they do read Christians.' In times which are becoming more and more unstable, we need more than ever to deepen our connection with God and to connect God with every part of our lives. The ancient practice of living by a Way of Life, rooted in scripture, modelled by the radical desert Christians and the Celtic missionaries, and being rediscovered by new monastic groups like the Community of Aidan and Hilda and ordinary local churches like the Ascension in Ealing, gives us an attainable, sustainable and utterly practical way of doing this. You too have a map and a compass here. It's time to go and explore.

> Stand at the crossroads, and look, and ask for the ancient paths, where the good way lies; and walk in it, and find rest for your souls.
> JEREMIAH 6:16

Notes

1   Simon Reed, *Creating Community: Ancient ways for modern churches* (BRF, 2013).
2   Quoted in Alison Morgan, *Following Jesus: The plural of disciple is church* (Resource, 2015), p. 38.
3   Mark Ireland and Mike Booker, *Making New Disciples: Exploring the paradoxes of evangelism* (SPCK, 2015), p. 13.
4   Ireland & Booker, *Making New Disciples*, p. 21.
5   In Tony Pullen, *Making Disciples: How did Jesus do it?* (CWR, 2014), frontispiece.
6   N.T. Wright, *Colossians and Philemon* (Inter-Varsity Press, 1986), p. 70.
7   Michael J. Wilkins, *Following The Master: A biblical theology of discipleship* (Zondervan, 1992).
8   Andrew Roberts, *Holy Habits* (Malcolm Down Publishing, 2016), p. 51.
9   Mark Oxbrow, international director of Faith2Share, in the Church Mission Society newsletter, *The Call*, Winter 2017.
10 See **ceministries.org**.
11 See **pilgrimcourse.org**.
12 Morgan, *Following Jesus*, p. 136.
13 Reed, *Creating Community*, pp. 113–114.
14 My counterpart in the USA pointed out to me that for some of their members to visit the next nearest person would be the equivalent of me flying to Moscow!
15 See Simon Reed, 'Followers of the Way: Biblical foundations for monastic living,' in Ray Simpson, *High Street Monasteries: Fresh expressions of committed Christianity* (Kevin Mayhew, 2009), pp. 127–150.
16 Bede, *The Ecclesiastical History of The English People*, ed. Judith McClure and Roger Collins (Oxford University Press, 1999), p. 146.
17 In recent years, many people have become aware that there are books about Jesus not included in the New Testament but also referred to as gospels. The four in the New Testament all take the form of ancient biography, a serious attempt to describe the life of an important person. The other books do not take this form and are

generally written a lot later, for which reason most biblical scholars do not regard them as reliable sources for understanding Jesus.

18 The WWJD (What Would Jesus Do?) wristbands have this one right.

19 It's also sometimes claimed that the KJV is the most accurate translation but this is incorrect. In later centuries, we have discovered more Hebrew and Greek manuscripts which allow us to improve on some errors in older translations.

20 John Goldingay, *The Old Testament For Everyone* series (SPCK, 2010–2016) and Tom Wright, *The New Testament For Everyone* series (SPCK 2002–2011).

21 Sermons of Calumbanus, I: Concerning the faith.

22 Bruce Stanley, *Forest Church: A field guide to a spiritual connection with nature* (Anamchara Books, 2014) is a really thought-provoking introduction, and a series of booklets called *Connecting with God in Creation* by Graham Booth are available direct from the Community of Aidan and Hilda.

23 Morgan, *Following Jesus*, p. 239.

24 Pullen, *Making Disciples*, p. 21.

25 David Cole, *The Mystic Path of Meditation: Beginning a Christ-centred journey* (Anamchara Books, 2013), pp. 53–58.

26 Richard Littledale, *Journey: The way of the disciple* (Authentic Media, 2017).

27 Mark E. Thibodeaux SJ, *Armchair Mystic: Easing into contemplative prayer* (St Anthony Messenger Press, 2001), p. 16.

28 Anglicans, Roman Catholics and other older churches have apps giving daily prayer and readings in the style of their tradition. Other examples of books of daily prayer are my own community's *Prayer Rhythms For Busy People* by Ray Simpson (Kevin Mayhew, 2005), the Northumbria Community's two-volume *Celtic Daily Prayer Book (William Collins, 2015), and Common Prayer: A liturgy for ordinary radicals* by Shane Claiborne, Jonathan Wilson-Hartgrove and Enuma Okoro (Zondervan, 2010).

29 *Celtic Prayer: Caught up in love*, from the Community of Aidan and Hilda and edited by David Cole (BRF, 2022), explores no less than 20 different ways to pray.

30 Mike Bickle, pastor of the International House of Prayer.

31 Although I've never implemented it completely, I use the 'workflow' system found in David Allen, *Getting Things Done* (Piatkus Books, 2001).

32 A highly regarded introduction to this is Mark Williams and Danny Penman, *Mindfulness: A practical guide to peace in a frantic world* (Piatkus Books, 2011), which explains how the process works and gives practical exercises, which can also be found on YouTube. Mindfulness as presented here is a neutral process contributing to mental and emotional well-being. An explicitly Christian version can be found at **christianmindfulness.co.uk**.

33 *Poems and Prose of Gerard Manley Hopkins*, ed. W.H. Gardner (Penguin Books, 1963), p. 27.

34 Green Christian is the first group I know who have developed a brief but full Way of Life with creation care at the centre (see **greenchristian.org.uk/way**).

35 See **arocha.org.uk** for their 'Living Lightly' ideas.

36 Ruth Valerio, *L is for Lifestyle: Christian living that doesn't cost the earth* (Inter-Varsity Press, 2nd edn. 2008) is a good place to start, and for those wanting to think more deeply about these issues and get involved on a larger scale, *Just Living: Faith and community in an age of consumerism* (Hodder & Stoughton, 2016).

37 **whatcar.com/news/true-mpg-most-and-least-efficient-cars-revealed/n14360.**

38 **climatestewards.org** explains how this works and payments can be made online.

39 In Matthew's Gospel, which has a typically Jewish desire to avoid using the name of God directly, this is called 'the kingdom of heaven', which has often misled Christians into thinking that Jesus' main concern was helping us go to heaven when we die. In fact, as the Lord's Prayer reminds us, Jesus was speaking about God's rule being expressed on earth as it is in heaven. See Tom Wright, *How God Became King* (SPCK, 2012), pp. 42–46.

40 One biblical historian who explicitly says he is not Christian writes: 'There should be no doubt at all that Jesus carried through a dramatic and successful ministry of exorcism and healing' (Maurice Casey, *Jesus of Nazareth: An independent historian's account of his life and teaching*, (T&T Clark, 2010), p. 275).

41 If you are interested in the scholarship, see Richard A. Burridge, *Imitating Jesus: An inclusive approach to New Testament ethics* (Eerdmans, 2007).

42 See John Wimber and Kevin Springer, *Power Healing* (originally Hodder & Stoughton, 1986).

43 Belden C. Lane, *The Solace of Fierce Landscapes: Exploring desert and mountain spirituality* (Oxford University Press, 1998).

44 When Jesus said, 'Blessed are the meek, for they will inherit the earth', he was almost directly quoting Psalm 37:11, but significantly replacing the word 'land' with 'earth'.

45 Russ Parker, *Healing Wounded History: Reconciling peoples and healing places* (Darton, Longman and Todd, 2001).

46 In Genesis 1:2 the Hebrew word *ruah* means both wind and Spirit.

47 Martin Laird, *Into The Silent Land: The practice of contemplation* (Darton, Longman and Todd, 2006).

48 In the Orthodox Christian tradition this is known as the Jesus Prayer. A good place to learn more about it is in Simon-Barrington Ward, *The Jesus Prayer* (BRF, 2022).

49 If you've already read *Creating Community*, you may notice that this waymark has been rewritten. At a recent Community of Aidan and Hilda meeting, we decided that ideas about 'spiritual warfare' in our original wording were confusing or controversial to many Christians, and that 'intercession' is actually a difficult term to define in relation to prayer.

50 Wright, *How God Became King*, p. 34.

51 Bede, *The Ecclesiastical History*, p. 135.

52 This of course leads us into the further debate about what the Bible means by marriage and, again, without getting into a complex discussion, it is arguably less obvious than we might think!

53 Laura Jane Grace with Dan Ozzi, *Tranny: Confessions of punk rock's most famous anarchist sellout* (Hachette Books, 2016), p. 11.

54 Rebecca Manley Pippert, *Out of The Saltshaker: Evangelism as a way of life* (Inter-Varsity Press, 1979).

55 For a brilliant fresh perspective on what our basic message is, and how it really is about telling people something not selling them something, see Tom Wright, *Simply Good News: Why the gospel is news and what makes it good* (SPCK, 2015).

56 Letters of Julian 22, *To Arsacius, High-priest of Galatia*.

57 See **stopthetraffik.org**.

58 Bob Holman, 'Keir Hardie', *Third Way* (November 1992), p. 21.

59 Uinseann Ó Maidín OCR, *The Celtic Monk: Rules and writings of early Irish monks* (Cistercian Publications, 1996), p. 46.

60 *St Benedict's Rule for Monasteries*, trans. Leonard J. Doyle (Liturgical Press, 1948).

61   In most traditional communities chastity, which means being faithful to your partner, is interpreted as celibacy, which means a commitment to singleness.

62   A good practical guide to doing this is Christian A. Schwarz, *The 3 Colors of Ministry: A Trinitarian approach to identifying and developing your spiritual gifts* (ChurchSmart Resources, 2001), available from Natural Church Development UK and Ireland (**ncd-uk.com**).

63   Angela Reith, *Who am I? Discovering your personality with the Enneagram* (Lion Publishing, 1999) is an excellent simple introduction, though now only available second-hand. Simon Parke's *The Enneagram: A private session with the world's greatest psychologist* (Lion Hudson, 2008) is a more thought-provoking way in.

64   See L. William Countryman, *Dirt, Greed, & Sex: Sexual ethics in the New Testament and their implications for today* (Fortress Press, 2007) for a really interesting examination of this.

65   Christopher Jamison, *Finding Sanctuary: Monastic steps for everyday life* (Weidenfeld & Nicolson, 2006), p. 76.

66   Ken Shigematsu, *God In My Everything: How an ancient rhythm helps busy people enjoy God* (Zondervan, 2013), p. 18.

67   Shigematsu, *God in My Everything*, p. 23.

68   I give some examples in *Creating Community*, chapter two.

69   Ray Simpson, *New Celtic Monasticism For Everyday People* (Kevin Mayhew, 2005, 2014).

70   Bede, *The Ecclesiastical History*, p. 116.

71   Warsan Shire, 'Home' (**seekershub.org/blog/2015/09/home-warsan-shire**).

SEPTEMBER–DECEMBER 2022

New Daylight

Sustaining your daily journey with the Bible

BRF

Included in this issue
Looking forward GORDON GILES
Hosea AMY BOUCHER PYE
Light and darkness STEPHEN RAND

New Daylight offers four months of daily Bible reading and reflection for everybody who wants to go deeper with God. It is ideal for those looking for a fresh approach to regular Bible study, and offers a talented team of contributors who present a Bible passage (text included), helpful comment and a prayer or thought for the day ahead. *New Daylight* is edited by Gordon Giles and is published three times a year in January, May and September. Available in regular and deluxe editions with large print, as a daily email and as an app for Android, iPhone and iPad.

New Daylight
Sustaining your daily journey with the Bible
£4.85 per issue, or subscriptions available both for print and app

brfonline.org.uk

In *Creating Community*, Simon Reed introduces us to a new but at the same time very old way of being church, which is based upon three core elements: a Way of Life, a network of Soul Friends and a rhythm of prayer. The book shows how the rediscovery of these elements by Christians today offers a vital key that opens up an ancient way for modern churches, one which not only helps to bring believers to lasting maturity but creates genuine and much-needed community in an increasingly fragmented world.

Creating Community
Ancient ways for modern churches
Simon Reed
978 0 85746 009 7 £8.99

brfonline.org.uk

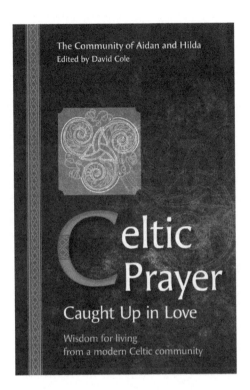

The Community of Aidan and Hilda
Edited by David Cole

Celtic
Prayer
Caught Up in Love

Wisdom for living
from a modern Celtic community

Even the most committed pray-ers can get stuck in a rut. Loved and familiar ways of praying can become dry and stale and it can be difficult to rekindle the spark, especially if you've only ever known a handful of ways to pray. But help is at hand in this wide-ranging and exciting new collection, edited by David Cole and with contributions from 30 members of the dispersed Community of Aidan and Hilda. *Celtic Prayer* explores 20 different ways of praying from the Celtic Christian tradition. Accessible and inspiring, it will refresh your spirit and draw you deeper into knowing God.

Celtic Prayer – Caught Up in Love
Widsom for living from a modern Celtic community
The Commnunity of Aidan and Hilda, edited by David Cole

978 1 80039 053 9 £12.99

brfonline.org.uk

Following the ancient rhythm of the Celtic year, these prayers, meditations and liturgies will help you focus on the natural flow of life as it changes around you. Based on the eight points of the Celtic year – the four season changes, and the four midpoints of each season – and moving from winter to spring, summer and harvest, each of the eight sections includes a liturgy for a full service, a week of daily readings, guided contemplations and a selection of prayers and blessings.

The Celtic Year
A rhythm of prayer and meditation for the eight points of the Celtic year
David Cole

978 0 85746 968 7 £8.99

brfonline.org.uk

The life stories of the Celtic saints are inspirational. They demonstrate great and unassuming faith, often in the face of insurmountable difficulties. In *Celtic Saints*, David Cole draws us to relate our own life journey and developing relationship with God into the life story of the Celtic saint of the day. A corresponding biblical text and blessing encourages and motivates us to transform our lives for today's world in the light of such historic faith.

Celtic Saints
40 days of devotional readings
David Cole
978 0 85746 950 2 £8.99

brfonline.org.uk

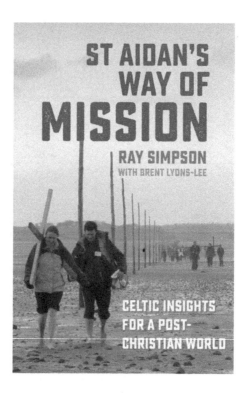

Surveying the life and times of Aidan of Lindisfarne, this book draws insights into missional approaches to inspire both outreach and discipleship for today's church. Ray Simpson shows that such figures from past centuries can provide models for Christian life and witness today. An author and speaker on Celtic spirituality with a worldwide reputation, he combines historical fact with spiritual lessons in a highly accessible style, with an appeal to a wide audience.

St Aiden's Way of Mission
Celtic insights for a post-Christian world
Ray Simpson
978 0 85746 485 9 £7.99

brfonline.org.uk

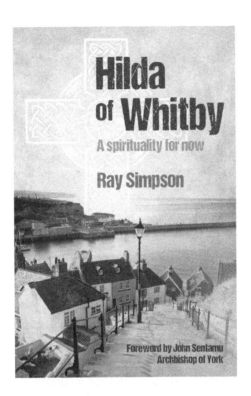

Hilda
of Whitby
A spirituality for now

Ray Simpson

Foreword by John Sentamu
Archbishop of York

In the dark and turbulent centuries after the Roman occupation of Britain and during the Anglo-Saxon colonisation, the light of heaven still shone through the work and witness of the monastic communities, 'villages of God', which dotted the land. One of the most remarkable figures of those times was Hilda of Whitby. Born and reared among warring pagan tribes, through the influence of Celtic saints and scholars she became a dominant figure in the development of the British Church. This book not only explores the drama of Hilda's life and ministry but shows what spiritual lessons we can draw for Christian life and leadership today.

Hilda of Whitby
A spirituality for now
Ray Simpson
978 1 84101 728 0 £7.99

brfonline.org.uk

Enabling all ages to grow in faith

Anna Chaplaincy
Living Faith
Messy Church
Parenting for Faith

100 years of BRF

2022 is BRF's 100th anniversary! Look out for details of our special new centenary resources, a beautiful centenary rose and an online thanksgiving service that we hope you'll attend. This centenary year we're focusing on sharing the story of BRF, the story of the Bible – and we hope you'll share your stories of faith with us too.

Find out more at **brf.org.uk/centenary**.

To find out more about our work, visit
brf.org.uk